A GUIDE TO

· ART ·
NOUVEAU
STYLE

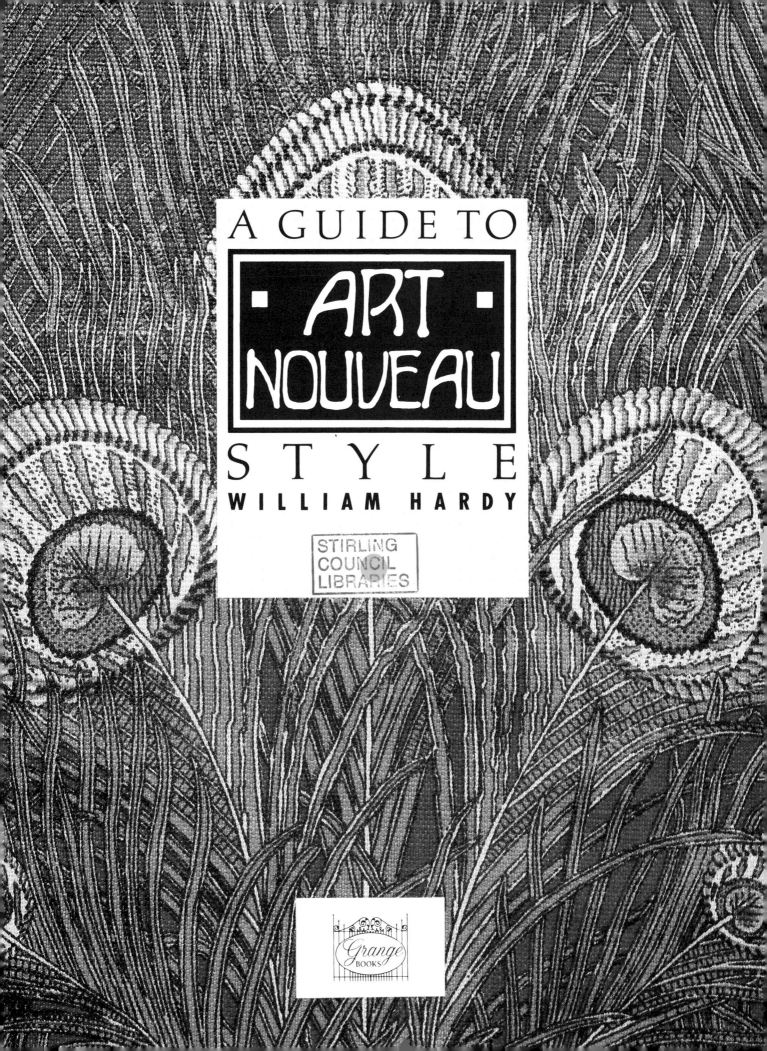

A GUIDE TO
·ART· NOUVEAU
STYLE
WILLIAM HARDY

Grange BOOKS

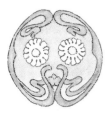

A QUANTUM BOOK

Published by Grange Books
an imprint of Grange Books Plc
The Grange
Kingsnorth Industrial Estate
Hoo, nr. Rochester
Kent ME3 9ND

709
034
HAR

ISBN 1-85627-832-8

QUMNOV

This book was produced
by Quantum Books Ltd
6 Blundell Street
London N7 9BH

Printed in Singapore by
Star Standard Industries Pte Ltd.

00606 4955

Picture Credits

E. T. Archives: **pp. 7, 11, 23(tl), 87, 110, 115**. Victoria and Albert
Museum: **pp. 9, 21(m & b), 109, 110, 111, 112-113, 114,
117(r), 119(b), 121, 122**. British Library: **pp. 10, 18(l)**. Werner
Forman Archive: **pp. 13, 22(3), 23(3)**. Bridgeman Art Library: **pp.
14(l), 15, 24-25, 25, 26-27, 58(l), 59(b), 66(t), 67, 69, 70,
72(b), 73, 78-79, 85, 97(t & bl), 102(3), 107(r), 116, 118,
119(tr), 120, 123**. William Morris Gallery: **p. 14(r)**.
Woodmansterne: **pp. 16, 18(r)**. Angelo Hornak: **pp. 19(l & r), 20,
21(t), 29, 30(t), 31, 32(m), 44(l), 45, 46(b), 50, 63, 65, 86,
88(l)**. Historisches Museum der Stadt Wien: **p. 27**. Architectural
Association: **pp. 30(b), 32(l), 34(2), 35, 37(2), 38, 40(r),
42-43, 43, 44, 46(t), 46-47, 58-59**. John Vaughan: **pp. 32(r),
33 (tr & br), 61, 64, 95**. Arcaid: **pp. 33(l)**. AISA: **pp. 36, 37(b),
38, 39, 40 (l & m), 41**. Josephine Bacon: **p.44 (tr)**. Sotheby's: **pp.
49, 53, 60(t), 68(b), 71, 107(l), 117(l)**. Musée des Arts
Décoratifs: **p. 51, 54, 55(b), 56(m), 56-57, 57(t), 99,
100-101, 104(l), 106(r)**. Gilbert Margin/Musée de l'Ecole de
Nancy: **p. 52, 53, 88(r)**. G. Dagli Orti: **pp. 55(r), 96, 97(br)**.
Christies: **pp. 56(t & b), 59(t), 60(b), 77, 80, 81, 82, 89(2),
90-91, 91(2), 92-93, 104(r), 106(l), 119(tl)**. Hubert Josse,
Paris: **pp. 57(b), 70-71, 94**. John Jesse & Irina Laski: **pp. 66(b),
68(t), 72(r), 73(l), 75, 76, 77, 83(l), 90(2), 92(l)**.
Hinous/Connaissance des Arts: **pp. 103, 105**.

Key: b—bottom; **l**—left; **m**—middle; **r**—right; **t**—top

CONTENTS

INTRODUCTION

Part of the French section of the Paris Exposition Universelle of 1900. Whilst technology advanced, the quality of design had stagnated or even regressed. Bombastic, clumsy, revivalist pieces such as this furniture horrified such critics as Ruskin and Morris.

RIGHT: *Embroidery by
Hermann Obrist. Here
is the purest
expression of the Art
Nouveau love of an
undulating line. Obrist
has taken his
inspiration from plant
life (roots, leaves and
flowers all being
discernable here) but
has developed the
forms into an
elaborate "whiplash"
pattern.*

 The essence of Art Nouveau is a line, a sinuous extended curve found in every design of this style. Art Nouveau rejected the order of straight line and right-angle in favour of a more natural movement Whether these lines were used in realistic depictions of natural forms or as abstracted shapes evoking an organic vitality, the emphasis was on decorative pattern and also flatness, a surface on which this concern for the linear, the line of Art Nouveau, could be developed. Solidity, mass, permanence, any connection with weight or stability and stillness ran counter to the Art Nouveau style. The insubstantiality of line was best exploited in light malleable materials, or those that could be fashioned to appear so. It was, in essence, a graphic style of decoration that was transferred onto a variety of solid objects. This curving, flowing line brought with it a feeling of airy lightness, grace and freedom.

Nature was the ultimate source book of the Art Nouveau artist, particularly the plant world, for many artists had a scientist's depth of knowledge of botany. Flowers, stems and leaves were chosen for their curving silhouettes. Naturally, lilies, irises and orchids were favoured, although any and every form, from palm fronds to seaweed, offered potential for development into an animated pattern. Insects and birds of colour and grace lent themselves to the same stylizing and refining process — dragonflies, peacocks, swallows, or creatures such as snakes or greyhounds. These decorative possibilities could also be developed from the curves of the female body, particularly when combined with long, loose, flowing hair which could be arranged into a fantasy of curls and waves. As the style developed, the quest for more novel forms grew.

Art Nouveau developed in the late 1880s and was at its creative height in the subsequent decade. By 1905 it had declined into being a much diluted ingredient in commercial design, soon to be replaced by an aesthetic felt to be more in keeping with the new century.

However, Art Nouveau itself owed much of its own popularity to its modernity, as reflected in the French term for the style which has since become universal.

The 19th century had seen enormous changes in society in both Europe and America, with the spread of industrialization resulting in the creation of great wealth concentrated on the new industrial and commercial cities. The mass-production methods of factories not only created a whole new class of workers but also a vast range of goods more widely available than ever before. Simultaneously, advances in technology — trains, steamships and the telegraph — were easing the problems of communication. The world had changed, yet there was no corresponding change in the styles employed to shape its appearance. In the design of everyday objects, just as in the design of buildings, the new age was offered continual revivals of old styles: Classical, Gothic, Renaissance, Baroque or Louis XV. Art Nouveau was the first style that did not seem to have its roots sunk deeply into European history. Instead it seemed to be the first truly new style of the century, despite the fact that it did not emerge until the closing decades. This helps to explain the fervour with which it was pursued and the rapidity of its spread.

The characteristic curving forms of Art Nouveau first appeared in England, yet they were to spread rapidly throughout Europe to a wide range of cities, each with a distinctive interpretation of the style: Paris and Nancy in France, Munich, Berlin and Darmstadt in Germany, Brussels, Barcelona, Glasgow and Vienna all become focal points for the style that was soon universal in Europe, and — with centres in New York and Chicago — equally influential in America. At the time, this range of regional styles resulted in some confusion as to terminology as well as sources. Often it was the theme of modernity that was to provide a name — 'Art Nouveau' and 'Modern Style' in France, 'Modernismo' in Spain and 'Moderne Stile' in Italy — or else a simple reference to place as with 'Belgische Stil' (Belgium Style) in Germany or 'Stile Inglese' in Italy. There was no clear idea as to a common origin, nor shared characteristics, until the style was in its decline. Only with hindsight has a more coherent view of the period been formed.

However, some contemporary terms for the style do throw light upon the way the style was disseminated, and serve to stress its internationalism. The term itself, 'Art Nouveau', derives from the Parisian shop of the same name run by a German emigré, Samuel Bing. Bing had been trading for ten years in Japanese art when, in 1895, he re-opened his premises as 'La Maison de l'Art Nouveau' and started to show the work of

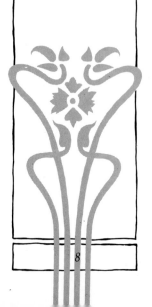

●

LEFT: *A cover by Otto Eckmann for the German periodical Jugend. The title itself appears in a typically fluid Art Nouveau script.*

1897 · 4. SEPTEMBER · **JUGEND** · II. JAHRGANG · NR. 36

JVGEND

Münchner illustrierte Wochenschrift für Kunst und Leben. — G. Hirth's Verlag in München & Leipzig.

RIGHT: Pan *from Berlin
covered the same
combination of visual
arts and literature as*
Jugend *did from
Munich.*

contemporary designers as well as painters and sculptors. This mixture of gallery, shop and showroom became the Parisian base for the new style, encouraging Bing to commission works for the shop and to promote his artists and craftsmen abroad. Bing's reputation as the impressario of Art Nouveau was sufficient for him to be allotted an entire pavilion for his own designers at the Paris Exposition Universelle of 1900. Another Italian term for the style, 'Stile Liberty', was a tribute to the London department store of the same name that sold the designs of progressive British craftsmen.

This mixture of commerce and art, so suitable for the Art Nouveau interest in household artefacts, was not restricted to a few enlightened retailers, but is best seen in the way the style spread through the great international trade fairs of the era. These events were products of the great age of industrialization, for they were descended from the 1851 London Great Exhibition, housed in the Crystal Palace, which had been held to demonstrate the possible applications of new technology. These exhibitions soon became an increasingly important feature of international commerce, at which the new styles of decorative art could be displayed. Particularly important events in the development of Art Nouveau were the international exhibitions of 1889 and 1900 in Paris, and of 1902 in Turin, while that of 1905, held in Liège, marked the end of the style's importance. Emulating the success of these commercial exhibitions were a number of international Fairs specifically devoted to the arts, such as

those of 1897 in Munich and Dresden, and a second Dresden show in 1899. Supporting these large events were innumerable smaller exhibitions of craft guilds and progressive groups of artists in Europe and America which reflected a widespread interest in new styles in every art form.

The depth of interest among the public in the new fashions in art, and particularly the decorative arts, was also reflected in the huge numbers of new magazines and periodicals devoted to these trends which appeared in the Art Nouveau era. The German version of the style, 'Jugendstil', even derived its name from the influential Munich-based journal *Jugend* (youth), while also sometimes being called 'Studiostil' after the widely read English, and later American, periodical *The Studio*. Equivalent publications were *Pan* from Berlin and *Ver Sacrum* from Vienna. The German language periodicals also included contemporary literature, poetry and criticism, but as in all such journals of the time the main coverage of the new style came not in specific articles but in the actual design of the publication itself. The title-page, typeface and illustrations were all the work of Art Nouveau graphic artists. Such periodicals had a wide circulation beyond the limited circle of craftsmen, but there existed too journals such as the influential *Art et Décoration* from Paris which concentrated more exclusively on the decorative arts, and included many photographs. Through exhibitions, shops, galleries and magazines the Art Nouveau style spread rapidly throughout Europe and America, both feeding off and stimulating the public's interest.

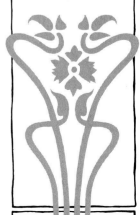

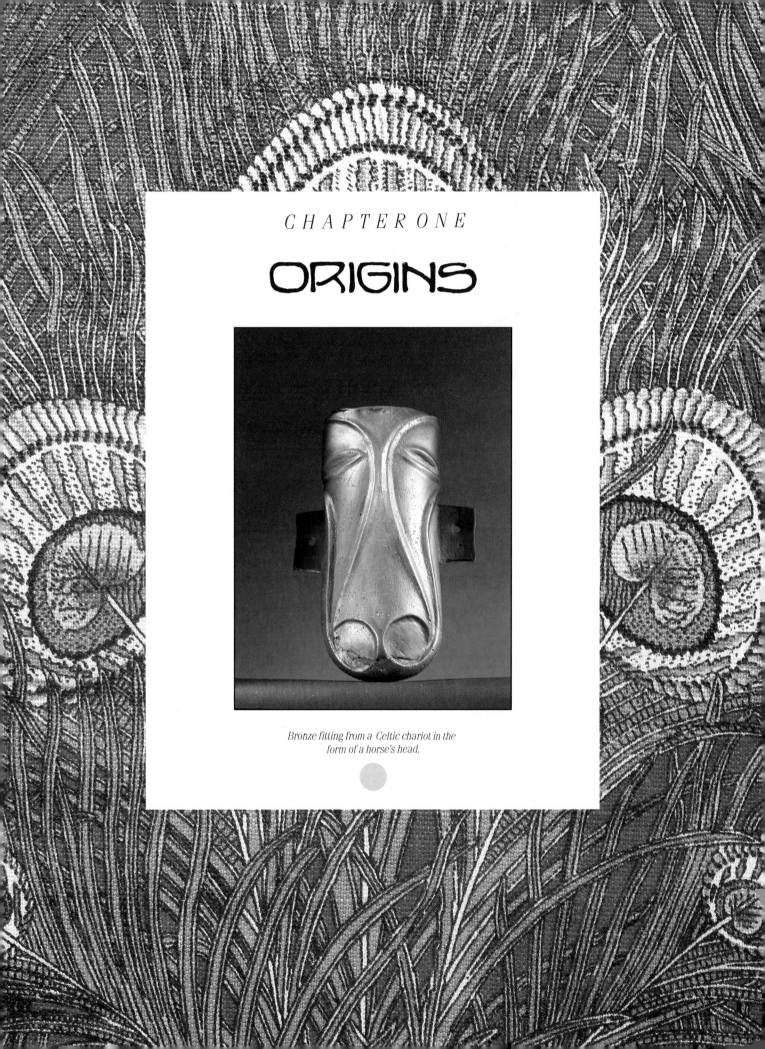

CHAPTER ONE

ORIGINS

Bronze fitting from a Celtic chariot in the
form of a horse's head.

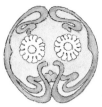

i once a king and chief · now am the tree-barks thief :

ever twixt trunk and leaf · chasing the prey ·

The origins of the Art Nouveau style are to be found in Victorian England. Here one discovers not only the sinuous decorative line that was to characterize the appearance of the style, but also the ideas that were to become its theoretical base. The Great Exhibition of 1851 had been held, not only to advertise new technology and promote trade, but also to advertise what were held to be examples of well designed objects. Some of the profits from the event went into the foundation of the Victoria and Albert Museum in London, whose purpose was to encourage a further interest in the decorative arts by means of its exemplary displays. A general climate of interest in the subject had been created, but the standards of the Exhibition were harshly criticized by the influential writer on art, John Ruskin.

Ruskin abhorred the products of mass-production and called for a return to craftsmanship inspired by a romantic view of the Middle Ages. He rejected as artificial the division that had arisen between the so-called fine arts and the decorative arts, pointing out that Michelangelo's great Sistine Chapel ceiling had in fact been primarily a work of decoration. By revitalizing the crafts, Ruskin hoped to develop an alternative to what he saw as the horror of factory labour, as well as improving the aesthetic quality of everday objects.

FAR LEFT
A Morris tapestry of 1885. Morris' inspiration lay partly in the natural world, and his depictions of plants, animals and birds are all well-observed but simplified and integrated into the overall design.

LEFT: *The Strawberry Thief, a Morris textile design of 1883. Curving natural shapes are symetrically ordered, unlike the more abandoned developments of Art Nouveau.*

CENTRE LEFT: *William Morris in 1877 when the Arts & Crafts movement that he had created was beginning to revolutionize English design.*

He advised craftsmen and architects to return to nature for their forms, rejecting the historicism of Victorian revivalism and anticipating the work of the Art Nouveau architects Horta, Guimard and Gaudí.

Ruskin's ideas were taken up by his disciple, the craftsman, poet, pamphleteer, printer, erstwhile painter and architect, William Morris. Ruskin's friends were the painters of the Pre-Raphaelite group and Morris began his career, firstly as a painter, as a follower of the group's dreamy interpretation of the medieval past. However, Morris had a more practical view of that period when it came to his attempt to recreate its idyll of painters, architects and craftsmen working together, often on the same tasks: in 1861 he founded a company to produce the type of objects he wanted to see in every home — this became Morris & Co. Morris was able to effect a genuine bridging of the divide between artists and craftsmen by employing his friends among the Pre-Raphaelite painters to decorate cabinets and bureau, and to design tapestries, fabrics and chairs. Morris' company was able to produce a complete range of goods to furnish the home, in a uniform style, to achieve an overall harmony of effect. In this, he anticipated the versatility of the Art Nouveau artist/craftsman.

RIGHT: *Morris & Co. provided a complete interior through versatility in all the crafts. Here, in the Honeysuckle room at Wightwick Manor, the wallpaper, carpet, tiling and furniture are all by Morris. They combine traditional simplicity with echoes of the medieval past.*

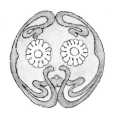

●

RIGHT: *Title page for Mackmurdo's* Wren's City Churches

FAR RIGHT: *Morris painted glass from Wightwick Manor. The central figure of Chaucer emphasizes the medieval inspiration for Arts & Crafts stained glass.*

The actual appearance of these goods was often reminiscent of medieval models, particularly in furniture, but in fabrics, carpets, wallpaper and decoration the Morris style derived largely from natural sources, inspired by plant, bird and animal forms. The use of hand-crafted, natural materials made these goods too expensive for ordinary people, yet despite this Morris still hoped that his products would become widespread enough to improve the quality of the lives of as many people as possible. Like Ruskin, he hoped to free the working man from the drudgery of factory labour and, through craftsmanship, enable him to gain pleasure from his work. Morris' ideals became polarized into socialism, which he espoused with increasing vigour toward the end of his life. In 1888 he established the Arts and Crafts Exhibition Society through which his work and that of his associates was displayed.

The example of the Morris Company encouraged other similar enterprises in Britain, usually referred to under the general term 'Arts and Crafts Movement'. Chief among these was the Century Guild, formed in

1884 by Arthur Mackmurdo. Influenced by the flowing, natural forms of Morris, Mackmurdo developed these shapes into elongated, increasingly elegant patterns and was the first to produce the characteristic vocabulary of Art Nouveau. The breakthrough is seen to be Mackmurdo's illustration for the title page of his book, *Wren's City Churches.* Here the flowers used by Morris, and roosters at either side framing the design, are drawn up into an artificial, stylized slenderness. The stems of the flowers undulate in an asymmetrical, rippling pattern like underwater plants animated by unseen currents. As early as 1883 Mackmurdo had created the sinuous, flame-like shapes that were to be the hallmark of Art Nouveau for the next 20 years.

Mackmurdo was undoubtedly the originator of a new direction, and the theme was rapidly developed in the work of the Century Guild and a similar pioneering body, the Art Workers' Guild, created by Walter Crane and Lewis Day in 1882. Through the Arts and Crafts Exhibition Society and the increasing output of Morris' followers, the work of the Arts and Crafts movement began to gain international recognition and the

medieval art of the mid-nineteenth century had emphasized the value of curving, organically inspired shapes seen in the architecture, sculpture and stained glass of the Middle Ages as a contrast to the rectilinear severity of classicism. Both Ruskin and Morris had turned to the medieval artists' study of nature as their inspiration and their interest was reflected in that of their contemporaries, the Pre-Raphaelite painters.

Dante Gabriel Rossetti and Edward Burne-Jones, leading Pre-Raphaelites, both designed and painted furniture for Morris as well as including specific details of dress and armour in their paintings. As this kind of historical appreciation of Gothic grew, so too did the awareness that this term encompassed a num-

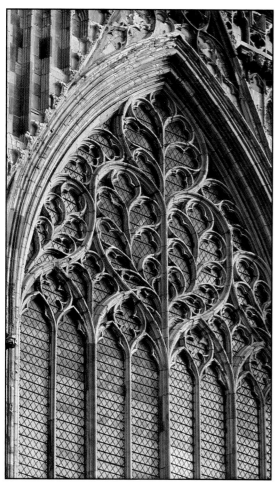

forms of Art Nouveau started to emerge to be developed elsewhere. However, it was not only a stylistic influence that was apparent but perhaps, more importantly, the ideals of Ruskin and Morris that acted as an inspiration to painters and architects to extend their activities into the decorative arts, to become craftsmen, and to revitalize society as a whole. Art Nouveau, as a style embracing all the arts, therefore owed its ultimate origin to the earlier English Crafts revival, with its concern for a unity of the arts allied to rather Utopian ideas of social renewal through handicrafts.

The first examples of the flowing forms of Art Nouveau occurred in the work of Mackmurdo's Century Guild. Not all stylistic features can be traced so easily to one source, nor, despite the apparent modernity of the movement, are they devoid of historical links. Despite the anti-revivalist, novel qualities of Art Nouveau, some of the strands of its complicated and extensive root structure were grounded in the revival of past styles. The Gothic revival served in some ways as an inspiration, for the fervent examination of

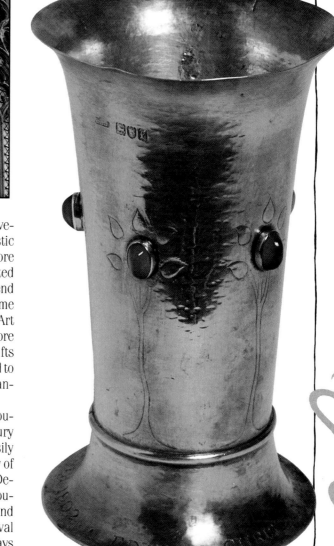

●

RIGHT: *The mirror room in the Amalienburg pavillion of the Schloss Nymphenburg, Munich for which French craftsmen produced a perfect expression of the rococo in 18th century Germany. The light, capricious elegance of the restless rococo line influenced Art Nouveau designers.*

ber of different styles, from the chaste, plain lines of its early period to the flamboyant fantasy of later medieval art. It was this form of the style that was to inspire the Art Nouveau. Stained glass, too, immediately reminiscent of the Middle Ages and revived by the Arts and Crafts workers, was also to play an important part in Art Nouveau design. The late Gothic style was plundered not to afford pedantic historical details, but as a sourcebook for new ideas.

Viollet-le-Duc differed from Ruskin in his acceptance of new industrially-produced materials in art, particularly the use of iron in architecture. Another Frenchman offers a striking parallel to both Ruskin and Morris: Léon de Laborde, the organizer of the French entry in the 1851 Great Exhibition. Laborde's report on the Exhibition criticized the gap that had been created between the arts and mechanically-produced artefacts. To correct this, he advised artists to concern themselves in future less with reviving the trappings of past styles and more with the design of everyday objects. These very Morris-like ideas were echoed by Viollet-le-Duc in his teaching at the Parisian Ecole-des Beaux-Arts, where he recommended far closer collaboration between all the arts, focusing on architecture, to produce a stylistically harmonious whole. With these two men, French Art Nouveau could look to its own theorists and writers for inspiration.

If flamboyant, late Gothic provided an example of the creative use of the past by the Art Nouveau, then so too did the inspired re-examination of the 18th century rococo style in France. This style had become one of the many open to the revivalists of the next century, but rather than resurrect it completely Art Nouveau observed its forms and characteristics with an independent eye. Rococo had been more broadly associated with use of a capriciously cavorting, light and delicate line as an ornament in all the decorative arts. This was very close to the line of Art Nouveau, and the connection became clear when, in France, the designers of the regional Nancy school began to incorporate references to rococo in their work. The common source of natural forms of plant and wave in both Art Nouveau and rococo made the blend harmonious. The rococo preference for light, high-keyed colour in interiors was also pursued by Art Nouveau, in reaction to the heaviness and solemnity of sombre Victorian interiors. While it was strongest in France, Munich had also been an important outpost of rococo in the 18th century, and it is no coincidence to find that the lightest, wittiest and most fanciful forms of Jugendstil were later to be found in that city in the work of Hermann Obrist (1863-1927) or August Endell(1871-1925).

LEFT: A detail from the Amalienburg revealing the curling leaf forms of rococo.

BELOW LEFT: Viollet-le-Duc's interest in the Gothic combines with a fascination for the use of iron in this design for vaulting. The elaborately-moulded brackets supporting the iron columns, and the openness of the interior made possible by the new materials, both anticipate subsequent developments in Art Nouveau.

BELOW: Iron is used here not only as a decorative element on the balconies but also as a structural framework, as can be seen from the buttresses dividing the shop windows, in this illustration to Viollet-le-Duc's Entretiens.

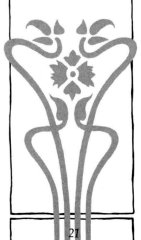

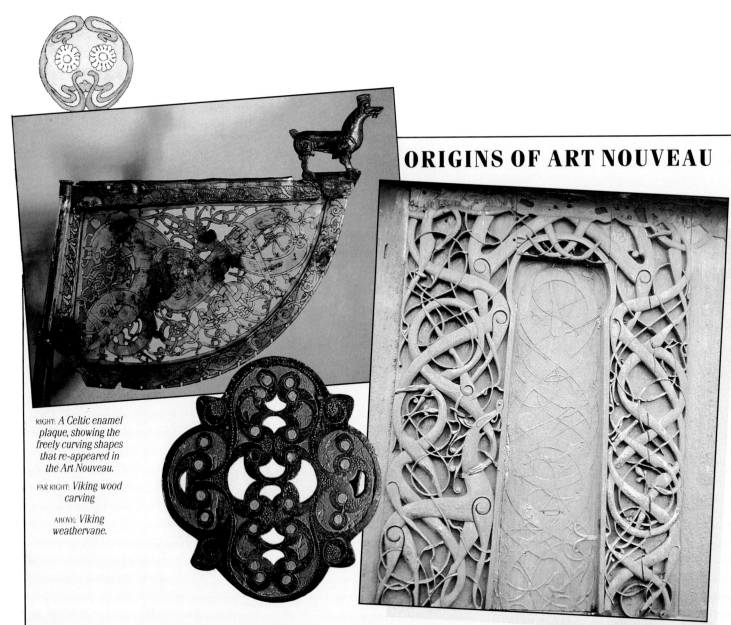

RIGHT: *A Celtic enamel plaque, showing the freely curving shapes that re-appeared in the Art Nouveau.*

FAR RIGHT: *Viking wood carving*

ABOVE: *Viking weathervane.*

Some stylistic revivals of the 19th century were partly inspired by the growing nationalism of the time, which was tinged, as ever, by a romantic idea of the past. Some of these revivals of national artistic consciousness also percolated into Art Nouveau, and helped to form its many regional variations. The revival of interest in early Celtic art became an important influence on the Glasgow school, and its most renowned figure, Charles Rennie Mackintosh. Celtic jewellery and the ancient gospel books of Durrow, Lindisfarne and Kells revealed precisely their elaborately curving and twisting decoration, the combination of stylization and

natural inspiration that typified Art Nouveau itself. More particularly, the use of lavish ornament confined within strict limits and contrasted with more open areas had strong parallels with the work of the Glasgow designers in all media. Interest in Celtic art was matched by enthusiasm for the similar ancient Irish and Anglo-Saxon styles, all evident in an example such as Liberty's 1900 range of jewellery, mysteriously named 'Cymric'.

An interest in early Nordic art in the Scandinavian countries emphasized their revived artistic vitality, and the intricate curves and spirals of this tradition found their way into the

local form of Art Nouveau, as in the designs of the Norwegian Henrick Bull. It was even occasionally termed the Dragon style in deference to its Viking source. Morris himself had also toyed with this style after several trips to Iceland, as well as translating the Viking sagas of that country.

Clearly Art Nouveau, although drawing from previous centuries, was far-removed from the rather naive and concentrated revivalism that had preceded it. With its capricious use of past and peculiar mixture of styles, Art Nouveau could not be anything other than a uniquely novel style. Its eclecticism extended to its strong roots in oriental art, and in particular

that of Japan. Japan was a relatively new discovery for the West, having been opened up to Western trade by the American Commander Perry in 1853. Perry stimulated the creation of a formal trade agreement in the following year, and the quantity of Japanese goods available in Europe and America steadily grew, as too did public interest in the highly sophisticated work of Japanese artists and craftsmen. Wood-cut prints became popular among the avant-garde artists, particularly in France, who discovered in them exciting new solutions to problems of composition and use of colour. Some of the leading figures of Art Nouveau began their involvement in

the decorative arts as champions of the new Japanese style. In London, Arthur Liberty set up business in a small shop trading in oriental goods before expanding his premises into the great turn-of-the-century department store, Liberty & Co. Before opening 'l'Art Nouveau', Bing had been one of the leading oriental dealers in Paris, and had formed an impressive personal collection. So to had one of his most important collaborators, the American designer and decorator Louis Comfort Tiffany, who later became one of the most prominent artists of Art Nouveau glassware.

The formal links between Japanese prints and Art Nouveau are strong. The emphasis on decorative line, creating flat, patterned work was immediately found to be sympathetic. Nor did the Japanese artists overburden their work with excessive ornamentation. Instead, they maintained a refined interplay between decoration and background, setting a light and elegant design against plain ground. The curving, flowing Japanese line was drawn from observation of nature, filtered through a developed design sense to create more abstracted forms and patterns with the precise degree of artificiality that the Art Nouveau artists found so pleasing. These features combined to create a sense of delicacy, refinement and sheer stylishness that was the aim of every Art Nouveau craftsman.

The art of Japan became by far the greatest single oriental influence on Europe at the time, but 19th century interest in the exotic, parallel to the infatuation for the romance of the past, had also stimulated a renewed interest in other cultures.

Java was one of the Dutch colonies at this time, and as Holland became a centre of Art Nouveau, Javanese art became a noticeable influence upon the Dutch form of the style. Javanese batik work, a form of textile printing using wax, was the most transportable art form and one whose exotic, flat patterns was of particular interest. The influential Dutch painter, Jan Toorop, made use of such patterns as well as of the distinctive insect-like stick puppets of Java. His 'Three Brides' is a highly stylized work that owes much of its disturbing elegance to this source, largely unknown thoughout the rest of Europe. Besides Japan and Java, Art Nouveau craftsmen also studied art of the Muslim world which had a similar tendency toward the abstraction of natural shapes and the creation of flat, rhythmic patterns. Art from Persia, Turkey and North Africa occured as occasional exotic influences.

ABOVE RIGHT: *Wind-blown waves by the master Japanese print maker Hiroshige whose ability to create an effective composition through flowing expressive line and a combination of simple flat shapes inspired the painters and designers of late 19th century Europe.*

BELOW FAR RIGHT: *An Indonesian stick puppet used in shadow theatre. The Dutch painter and designer, Jan Toorop, used the attenuated forms of these figures in his art.*

ABOVE FAR RIGHT: *The intricate, curving pattern of these Thai figures also supplied European artists with decorative ideas.*

BELOW RIGHT: *A medieval Persian flask whose twisted handles and irridescent surface are typical of the features that fascinated the exponents of Art Nouveau.*

BELOW RIGHT: *J. McNeil Whistler's Peacock room including his own painting* La Princesse du Pays du Porcelaine *over the fireplace. Whistler based himself in late 19th century London but was familiar with artistic and literary life in Britain and France. An eminent dandy in the manner of Oscar Wilde, he also used his paintings to evoke moods in a manner comparable to the work of Symbolist poets. Here his concern is to create a complete environment, designing all the elements himself. Of particular interest are the peacocks on the gold-painted window shutters whose extravagant plumage is treated with Art Nouveau sweeping linearity.*

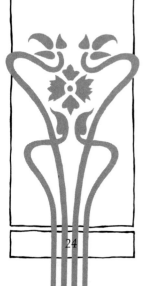

While Art Nouveau drew stylistic inspiration from the orient, and to some degree from the past, it was also firmly embedded in its own time. Socially, economically and intellectually, it was created by the needs of the age. Europe was at its wealthiest before the disasters of the two world wars; the upper and middle classes in every country were prepared to spend surplus income on expensively-produced objects for the home which made their owners feel themselves to be discerning and stylish.

The techniques and materials employed in the production of these goods were very often the result of 19th century technological progress. This applied not only to the more dramatic products of industrialization, such as the use of iron architecture, but to new firing and glazing processes in ceramics and glassware, electroplating in metalwork and the use of the electric light. The technological aspects of process or material might not be stressed by the Art Nouveau designer as he wrapped metallic ivy around an electric lamp or turned his ironwork gate into a medievally-inspired dragon, but, despite a nostalgia for craftsmanship, designers nevertheless placed the products of the style firmly in the industrialized age.

There was a strong connection between the decorative arts and literature throughout Europe. All the arts were retreating from the aggressive realism of the previous decades into a more creative and imaginative response to nature. In painting, this took the form of a reaction to the truthful rendering of the visual sensation of the Impressionists, in literature a reaction to the social realism of Zola or Dickens. Instead, there was a new emphasis on subjective inspiration.

Music as a non-descriptive art form was a common inspiration, but visual artists also turned to writers in order to explore a world of feelings and moods. More artists began to illustrate works of literature or refer to them in their work. This applied to Art Nouveau craftsmen too. Emile Gallé inscribed furniture and glassware with favourite quotations from contemporary poets, pieces of pottery or jewellery were given semi-literary titles, mythological themes were alluded to, all in an attempt to endow the work with extra significance.

The Symbolist school of literature placed greater emphasis on evocation of moods or emotions, often intangible and mysterious, rather than factual description. The Art Nouveau artist pursued a similar path when he abstracted forms from nature, intending to communicate the essence of a flower by its gentle lines and fresh colour, rather than by minute description. Poets such as Mallarmé also stressed the artificiality of their work and its aesthetic qualities, and tried to emulate the ornament and decoration of the artist by intricate language and the use of unusual words.

For the self-styled decadents, the pursuit of excellence in art was the most important thing in life, for beauty was more important than morality. Everything might be sacrificed in order to attain a beautiful result. This extreme aestheticism reached its peak in the figure of Oscar Wilde, whose libel action and subsequent trial in 1895 for homosexuality discredited the fashion for decadence in England.

In France, the most extreme dandy of this type was Count Robert de Montesquiou, a great patron of Art Nouveau craftsmen, whose every possession had to be of the most exquisite beauty and quality. This was a strange, ironic mutation of Morris' theory that the homes and lives of poorer people could be improved by the better quality of their possessions. Montesquiou was immortalized as the decadent aristocrat, Des Esseintes, in the novel by Huysmans *A Rebors*, which consists of lengthy descriptions of the beautiful objects which surrounded the hero. This degree of luxury and aesthetic commitment to the quality of the

smallest possession sustained the resurgence of the decorative arts during the Art Nouveau era.

The relationship between Art Nouveau and contemporary painting was more ambiguous and complex. Although the flat, flowing shapes of Art Nouveau are first discernable in Mackmurdo's work in England, they also appear independently in French painting of the time. Reacting to Impressionism, Paul Gauguin began to develop his own form of symbolist painting, concentrating on large, flat, interlocking areas of colour strongly outlined by emphatic, curling contours. In this he was as much influenced by Japanese woodcuts as subsequent Art Nouveau artists were to be. The strongest example of this, the *Vision After the Sermon* of 1888, was heralded by him as the beginning of the cloissonist or enamel style, paying tribute to an influence from the decorative arts; for enamel work, like stained glass, consists of flat areas of strongly-outlined colour.

Gauguin's style was well-known to those Art Nouveau craftsmen who began as painters, but Gauguin himself cannot be described as an Art Nouveau artist. Although there are similarities in style, Gauguin's personality was strong and he used these stylistic features to communicate a personal view rather than as a purely decorative feature. However, the followers of Gauguin, who in 1893 formed themselves into a group called the Nabis, seized upon the flat, decorative aspects of his style.

The Nabis knowingly blurred the distinction between fine and decorative arts. One of their number, Maurice Denis, made the famous statement that a picture 'is essentially a flat surface covered with colours assembled in a certain order'. Denis' paintings of this period do indeed appear like Art Nouveau designs, with their flat shapes, broad flowing curves and subject matter that is merely charming and decorative rather than interesting in its own right. It bears a close similarity to the embroidery of the Art Nouveau designer Henry Van de Velde, essentially a piece of decorative craft work. With a newfound Catholic faith to fire his painting, Denis later repudiated his flirtation with the principles of graphic art and Art Nouveau, but his work and those of his fellows Nabis reveal the closeness of the fine and decorative arts in the 1890's.

ORIGINS

•

BELOW LEFT: The Kiss, *by Gustav Klimt. The figures, and consequently the subject of the piece, become overwhelmed by his interest in pattern.*

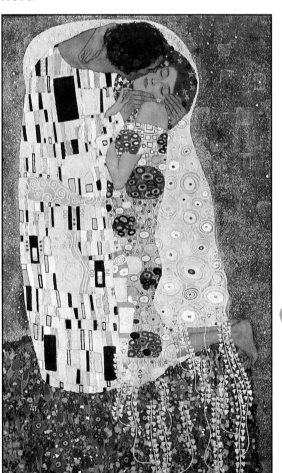

RIGHT: Le Divan Japonais, *poster by Henri de Toulouse-Lautrec. Working on a poster, Lautrec became a master of Art Nouveau design, whilst maintaining a more personal style in his paintings.*

FAR RIGHT: Emile Flöge *by Gustav Klimt. Here Klimt incorporates decorative elements into what is still a painterly work.*

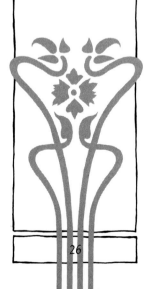

Painters who did not pursue Gauguin's style also explored similar areas. Pierre Puvis de Chavannes built a successful career on large mural paintings with a strong decorative element, consisting of muted colours and generalized, rather flat shapes of figures in landscape. Georges Seurat, who in many ways continued the exploration of the light effects and brushwork of the Impressionists, also became interested in the expressive possibilities of pure line, exploiting, in his later works, an equivalent of the whiplash contour of Art Nouveau decorators. The poster artist, Chéret, who also influenced Henri de Toulouse-Lautrec was a strong influence on Seurat at this time. Although Toulouse-Lautrec was also inspired by the impressionist Raoul Dégas, and painted similar cabaret and brothel scenes, he too was inclined to flatten shapes out and concentrate upon an expressive, meandering line. Toulouse-Lautrec also produced many successful posters which, with their curvilinear stylizations, simplifications and flowing, active lettering, deserve to be treated as masterpieces of Art Nouveau graphic art.

In some ways, the traditional view of painters being the serious experimenters and innovators whose creations inspire those of their colleagues in the minor decorative arts, can be seen to be true in the case of Art Nouveau, particularly in its relationship with Gauguin. However, the converse is also true, that the vitality and inventiveness of Art Nouveau designers inspired painters. Certainly many painters, sculptors and architects deserted their own specialities to work in the sphere of general design, which they felt to be both more lively and socially useful. Art Nouveau crafts were rapidly accepted as arts and displayed on an equal footing with painting, as in the pioneering exhibitions of the Vingt group in Brussels which influenced the development of Horta and Van de Velde.

It is easier to discuss a painter in terms of Art Nouveau influence, or of certain common characteristics shared with Art Nouveau, than it is to discuss an Art Nouveau painting. Since Art Nouveau is a term most accurately applied to the decorative arts, it implies some degree of judgement of a painter's subject matter if one classes his work as Art Nouveau. The example of Gustav Klimt typifies the dilemma. Klimt was an Austrian painter who had very close associations with Viennese designers and architects. As his style progressed, he became more influenced by their work, and by mosaics, until his figures became very flat and set into a background consisting of a purely decorative frieze of gold and abstract patterns. Klimt's subject matter retains its concentrated eroticism, which is the theme of his work as a whole, but he comes as near as a painter can to painting in Art Nouveau style.

CHAPTER TWO

ARCHITECTURE

A detail of the base of the Eiffel tower shows some of the ornament which embellishes what is still today a great feat of modern engineering.

ABOVE RIGHT: *The iron -and glass vaulting of Brighton Station typifies the use made of these materials by railway engineers before they entered the mainstream of Art Nouveau architecture.*

BELOW RIGHT: *The curling iron work of Victor Horta's Tassel House in Brussels.*

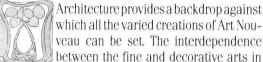

Architecture provides a backdrop against which all the varied creations of Art Nouveau can be set. The interdependence between the fine and decorative arts in Art Nouveau is best seen via the work of the major architects of the time, who required fittings in keeping with their domestic architecture while their fellow craftsmen needed the appropriate setting to display their work. From among the fine arts it is architecture that has the strongest technical, craft base, and when the conventional crafts were on the decline in the face of industrialization architects were at the forefront of their revival. William Morris, his colleague Philip Webb, and Arthur Mackmurdo were all trained architects. Many of the leaders of Art Nouveau were also architects: Horta, Guimard, Van de Velde, Behrens, Mackintosh, Gaudí, Gaillard and Grasset.

The architects of the Arts and Crafts movement looked back to a nostalgic pre-industrial era of simple brick and stone country dwellings, inspired by the rich tradition of English architecture, but the architecture of Art Nouveau began from an opposing premise. Instead of a reactionary rejection of the industrially-produced material of iron and glass, now more readily available and so dramatically demonstrated in the 1851 Great Exhibition in London, Art Nouveau architects eagerly embraced the possibilities these suggested. Art Nouveau architecture became an important basis for twentieth century developments, and opened the way to the modernist style.

The use of iron to provide strong and comparatively light frames for buildings was first developed in the architecture of the railways and other related industries. It was clear that its strength would inevitably lead to its use in more traditional architecture too, but in England, where iron had been most dramatically used, the development was tentative. Ruskin's distaste for industrial materials was a strong influence, and when iron was used its structural role was hidden as much as possible by the more conventional brick and stone. However, in France, Viollet-le-Duc had no qualms in recommending the open use of iron in his writings, realizing its suitability for the light, high vaults of his favoured Gothic style and, very significantly, suggesting ways in which it could be shaped to create foliage patterns to embellish its role as a structural element. This exploitation of the initial malleability of iron to create naturalistic ornament was to be of the greatest significance for Art Nouveau architects. In complete contrast to Ruskin, Viollet-le-Duc was excited by the industrial architecture he saw. The Chocolat Menier factory built outside Paris in 1871 prompted him to speculate in his *Entretiens sur l'ar-*

chitecture on the further uses of iron and to produce a design for the combination of iron and stained glass (again with recourse to Gothic), a combination whose lightness and colour recommended it to the proponents of Art Nouveau.

The great engineer, Gustave Eiffel, also carried the influence of English engineering to France. Eiffel was

●

LEFT: *The Solvay house façade, gently curving with large windows. The ironwork of the balconies and window mullions provides the decoration.*

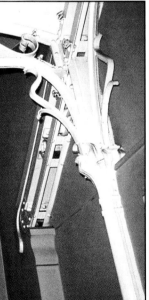

increasingly involved in the design of pavilions at the numerous international exhibitions, allowing more and more of the supporting metal frame to be revealed. It was for the Paris Exhibition of 1889 that his most famous and daring creation, the Eiffel Tower, was produced. When this was allowed to remain after the dismantling of the Exhibition it became an import-ant, if controversial, monument to the possibilities of the new medium. In the manner of Viollet-le-Duc, Eif-fel had also attempted to embellish his engineering masterpiece with some decorative flourishes in iron. The result is a compromise between English rectili-nearity and the Belgian and Spanish Art Nouveau extravagance.

The work of Viollet-le-Duc and Eiffel was in some ways carried on by the highly influential first Art Nouveau architect, the Belgian Victor Horta. That such architecture emerged in Brussels before Paris is a tribute to the highly-developed artistic climate of the Belgian capital. The foundation of the exhibiting Société des Vingt in 1884 had given Brussels a place among the main centres of Symbolist painting. In 1892, when les Vingt began including decorative art in their exhibitions, it was as a recognition of the change in emphasis in the arts associated with Art Nouveau. The same year, Horta began his Tassel House at 6 Rue Paul-Emile, and Art Nouveau architecture had begun in Brussels.

Horta's early work had been with his employer, the academically classical architect Alphonse Balat, who had built the imposing Musée Royal des Beaux-Arts. The Tassel House could not contrast more strongly with this ponderous official architecture. In the interior, Horta exposed the iron columns in the hall and stairwell that carried much of the building's weight, refusing to conceal them with brick or plaster. These slender forms were then given a treatment entirely Art Nouveau in character. Rather than mould them into a conventional Gothic or classical column, as had been done before in similar circumstances in industrial architecture, Horta shaped these supports to resemble the stems of some fantastic vegetation. At the capital level of the column he attached numerous twisting and turning metal fronds, as if the main column had sprouted fresh growths that were tender and malleable. The design of the metal was emphasized by wall-and-ceiling paintings of similar loosely-flowing tendrils, which were repeated in the mosaic pattern of the floor. These features and the pale colour scheme gave the building an air of freshness, vitality and movement. Horta even managed to give the walls of the main floor characteristics of their own by using moulded and shaped partitions. The less striking exterior of the Tassel House confirms the importance of the interior for Art Nouveau, where the artist could exert a more complete control, and it is the stairwell rather than the façade that is of most importance.

The fully-fledged Art Nouveau of the Tassel House had an immediate impact, and Horta began to develop his style through a number of commissions. The Hotel Solvay in Brussels, originally designed as a

VICTOR HORTA

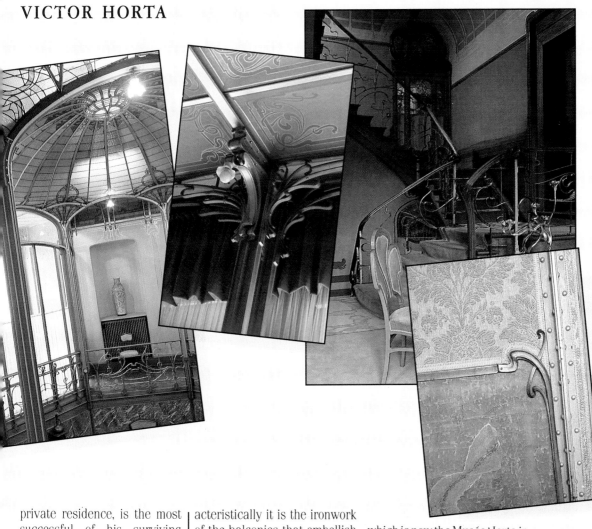

private residence, is the most successful of his surviving façades, in essence a gentle curve between two framing bays supported by iron columns and almost entirely glazed. Horta was eager to lighten the effect of his architecture as much as possible with large windows, wide doorways and open stairwells giving an impression of open, airy space to his interiors. Now that these devices have become more commonplace it is easy to overlook the refreshing effect these rooms must have had after the cluttered gloom of a Victorian interior. There is little decoration on the stonework of the Hotel Solvay exterior; char-acteristically it is the ironwork of the balconies that embellish it. The curving effect is contin-ued in the panels of the main door and in the interior with banisters, handles and light fit-tings, all designed by Horta. The latter are particularly success-ful, falling from the ceiling like inverted creepers whose flow-ers are the shades for the elec-tric light bulbs. Horta's attention to detail is such that all the fit-tings in the house, down to the furniture and the locks, continue the curvilinear theme. Not sur-prisingly, considering the degree of control over his envi-ronment which he exerted, Horta designed his own house, which is now the Musée Horta in Brussels.

Horta's most ambitious work of this period was the Maison du Peuple, a vast social centre, since demolished. In the large auditorium of this building Horta supported his structure upon a metal frame that was entirely exposed, a daringly modern device typically coun-terbalanced by the reassuringly smooth curves of the iron ribs, beams and balconies. The exte-rior, built almost entirely of metal and glass, again used a mixture of modern materials, with the more typically Art Nou-veau curving façade and a cer-tain fussiness of massed win-dow and balcony features. The Maison du Peuple, as a cultural and social centre for the work-ing classes, reveals Horta's involvement with socialism, appearing superficially at odds with the kind of refined elegance characteristic of his art and the influence of Morris' ideals. His use of English wallpaper in the Tassel House also emphasizes his debt to the Arts and Crafts movement and underlines the impetus from England that set Art Nouveau on its course in the early 1890s.

●

ABOVE RIGHT: *Detail of the Castel Béranger shows Guimard's fluid handling of metalwork. Note too the abstract forms of the stonework behind.*

BELOW RIGHT: *The entrance to Guimard's Castel Béranger where stone is carved to create the impression of a malleable material.*

Horta's influence was soon felt in Paris, where the leading French architect of Art Nouveau, Hector Guimard, acknowledged Horta as one of the originators of the new style, coupled modestly with his own name. While Horta limited his plant-like decoration mostly to interiors, and even there treated it with a certain coolness, Guimard allowed fantasy to dominate his work. At times, as in his furniture designs, he seemed to be deliberately challenging the accepted limitations of his medium, whether it was iron, wood, or stone. This kind of wilfulness finds its extreme form in the Spaniard Gaudí, but Guimard's roots are very French, based on the ideas of Viollet-le-Duc but without using any form of overtly Gothic style. The nearest Guimard came to this was in the rather self-consciously rustic chalets he produced, such as the Castel Henriette, with quaint, pitched roofs and a restless sense of movement in the forms of gables, doors and windows. The greater informality of out-of-town architecture is also well demonstrated in the Villa Henry Sauvage built for the designer Louis Majorelle, outside Nancy. The house, with its high gables, assertive asymmetry and details of chimney pots and balconies, approaches a fairytale whimsy. Only hinted at here, the verticality of Gothic was often very near the surface of French Art Nouveau architecture, as in the work of Charles Plumet who liked to use steeply-roofed dormer windows and pointed arches, or in the town house that the jewellery designer René Lalique created for himself by adapting the vocabulary of French châteaux architecture.

If Guimard's country villas had a sort of quaintness, then his Parisian work is more forceful. In building his own house on the Avenue Mozart he carved the stonework into the most dramatic forms, no longer simply just natural in origin, suggesting trees and plants, but exaggerated into a more artificial fantasy and elegance. Guimard's concern for detail was equal to that of Horta. In this house as well as in his major apartment block, the Castel Béranger, his designs in metalwork and stained glass are particularly notable. In these he created purely abstract forms, emphasized by the terracotta panels decorating the entrance of the building, which ooze and flow across the walls as if they were still molten.

However, it was Guimard's work for the Paris Métro that gave him most public prominence, and even resulted in a local variation, the style Métro, one of the many different names used to describe Art Nouveau. While the overhead structures of the Métro in the suburbs had been given a conventional treatment, incidently earning a decoration for their architect, Guimard was commissioned to produce shelters and

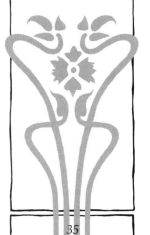

confronts one of the strangest variations of Art Nouveau, so firmly embedded in the peculiar local conditions that it is almost possible to see it as a purely local style. Yet, paradoxically, one of the strongest features of Art Nouveau was its very diversity. The remarkably different set of characters, linked by common Art Nouveau traits, sets the short-lived movement apart from the homogeneity of previous styles, arid and easily-transferred from master to pupil. The blossoming of Art Nouveau in Brussels, Barcelona, Glasgow, Munich, New York and so many other centres was a unanimous rejection of excessive uniformity.

Catalonia in particular had its own traditions. It was the wealthiest and most modern part of Spain, with its own industries and the thriving port of Barcelona, and was immensely proud of its trading history. These were vital to the Catalan identity at a time when the central government in Madrid was attempting to integrate the region more completely into Spain, partly by discouraging the use of the native Catalan language. In this context of spirited Catalan patriotism, Gaudí began his architectural career as a Gothic revivalist, but more specifically as a revivalist of the local Gothic style. This had its own element of fantasy, which Gaudí managed to emphasize through his study of the Moorish architecture of southern Spain and North Africa. To this, Gaudí added a knowledge of Viollet-le-Duc's work and the light, almost tent-like, forms of his iron-supported Gothic vaults, and of Ruskin, with his ideals of the unity of the arts and of architecture making use of colour and carving more for its effects.

Gaudí was fortunate enough to have an outstanding patron for much of his work in the local shipping magnate Don Eusebio Güell, whose wealth allowed for very ambitious schemes. Gaudí's development was slow at first, and his 1880s city mansion for Güell is largely inspired by Catalan Gothic, but for the two massive parabolic arches of the portals, swelling up to be filled by some of the most free-flowing ironwork decoration seen before Horta and Guimard. Perhaps inspired by the flowering of Art Nouveau in the rest of Europe, Gaudí's work of the 1890s began to develop into something unique, much more than just the sum of his early influences. Equally liberating must have been the scale on which he was invited to work by Güell. A development of workers' housing did not get very far but the centrepiece of a parallel scheme for a middle class neighbourhood, the Park Güell, exists today as a municipal park.

The Park Güell could be seen to be a rare opportunity for the Art Nouveau artist to display his art against its source. Since this was a landscaping commission,

LEFT: A Guimard entrance to the Paris Métro showing the characteristic lettering of the Art Nouveau style.

archways for the entrances to the underground sections. These were so startlingly Art Nouveau in their design that they provoked considerable controversy.

In keeping with the modernity of the new underground railway, Guimard restricted himself to the use of iron, enamelled steel and glass. The iron elements were produced in a large number of standard parts, making their assembly into a huge variety of differing arches and pavilions a tribute to Guimard's inventiveness and versatility. The treatment of the ironwork was typically curvilinear with barely a straight line to be seen in the whole design. Lamps sprouted from metal branches and the word 'Metropolitain' itself was carefully composed into harmonious Art Nouveau forms. Some of these ironwork shapes, although organic in feel, had an angular tension strangely reminiscent of bones and lacked the fluid grace of much of Guimard's interior designs, and of French Art Nouveau as a whole.

A typical Art Nouveau blend of rather esoteric revivalism and startling novelty is to be found in the work of Spaniard, Antonio Gaudí. In Gaudí's work one

•

RIGHT: *The interior of Gaudí's mansion for Don Eusebio Güell shows the architect's early interest in the ornate Gothic style.*

●

ABOVE LEFT: *The continuous bench that runs around the roof of the market in Gaudí's Güell Park.*

BELOW LEFT: *Detail of Wall of Gaudí's Parc Güell.*

●

RIGHT: *Details of the polychromatic decoration including the Güell monogram and coronet.*

Gaudí was able to employ the stylized, sinuous forms of Art Nouveau against the very natural shapes of the trees and flowers that had, in part, inspired them. Serpentine paths did, indeed, weave through the park, but the centrepiece was a vast covered market roofed in under a forest of massive columns. On the plateau created above this area, Gaudí placed benches, arranged in an almost continuous, undulating line from which the view could be enjoyed. The backs of the benches were decorated with a mosaic of broken tiles arranged, either in patterns or haphazardly, to create a dazzingly colourful display. The same theme was continued on the roofs of the pavilions within the park below. With further grottoes and concrete buttresses seemingly in the form of petrified treetrunks, the overall effect of the park is that of a strange mixture of the subterranean and maritime, perhaps appropriate for a city set between the mountains and the sea. The forms used within this fantastic realm have been justly likened to enormously magnified versions of the Art Nouveau creations of Horta and Guimard, amplifying the air of strange, in this case oversized, biological mutations. An interest in polychromatic effects gained through a combination of media, as in the Park Güell, was a frequent concern of Art Nouveau with characteristic ensembles of wood, metal and stained glass, and it was pursued by Gaudí in his Casa Battló

apartment block of 1905-7. This commission involved remodelling an existing block and the emphasis was inevitably on the façade. Gaudí had to contend with rectangular windows, already a part of the building and totally at odds with the shapes of Art Nouveau. In order to distract attention from them as well as exploit the shimmering light of a coastal city, coloured tiles were again used to create a flowing pattern throughout the façade, which was finished with a steep roof of tiles coloured orange to blue-green. These brilliant colour effects enabled Gaudí to move away from the more symmetrically-composed façades of the neighbouring houses. By means of a rather exotic turret and the fabric-like folds of the roof, the Casa Battló also managed to rise above its companions in the street. Gaudí reworked the base by using a stone cladding, whose flowing lines and softly-modelled protuberances seemed closer to underwater life than architecture. Some of the remaining windows of the upper storeys received bizarrely shaped iron balconies, somewhat resembling fish skeletons. While the Casa Battló was concerned with a rather two-dimensional presentation, the Casa Milá apartments, completely designed by Gaudí, received a much more plastic, virtually sculptural, treatment. Rapidly named La Pedrera, the quarry, by the locals, Casa Milá seems to allude to many natural sources. Like a cliff face or a

LEFT: *For the housing development around the Güell Park. Gaudí designed the church of Santa Coloma de Cervello, whose perilously leaning interior columns create an uneasy sense of movement. Equally distinctive is Gaudí's furniture. The insect-like forms of wood and iron intensify the impression of restlessness, furthered by the broken light from the stained-glass windows.*

rock outcrop eroded by wind into a collection of grottoes and tunnels, it seems to have been converted to human habitation only at some late stage in its history. Even in plan it appears like some cellular organism rather than the work of an architect, and the internal structure, was indeed, only arrived at at a late stage by the use of partitions. As Gaudís career developed, it is probable that he increasingly abandoned architectural drawings and worked at first hand with his craftsman, like a latter-day William Morris. Certainly he became was much less reliant on iron and glass than Horta or Guimard as seen in the Casa Milá. Instead, the effect of erosion is produced by careful carving of each block of the stone façade. In total contrast to this softness is the ironwork of the balconies which is moulded into intricately-twisted plant forms, like seaweed hanging from the cliff face before the next wave breaks upon it. Such marine analogies seem most applicable when one is faced by this huge block which

seems to flow around the street corner, softening the grid plan of the streets in this part of the city. However, there are no natural parallels for the forms of the chimney pots that crown the building. These spiralling shapes seem more like giant works of confectionery, and are the epitome of the free cuau carried into massive, spiralling, three dimensions.

Gaudí's great Barcelona church, the still-unfinished Sagrada Familia, occupied him for his entire career and, like the Casa Milá, is an example of extreme Art Nouveau fantasy enlarged into monumental three dimensions. It, too, is that typical combination of the reactionary and the revolutionary, stemming from Gaudí's extremely devout, rather anachronistic Roman Catholicism, here given a form of unique novelty: Gothic seen through the Art Nouveau eyes of the late nineteenth century. Like the Casa Milá, it invites comparison with natural rock forms. It has been suggested that one of the most important

LEFT: *The Casa Battló interiors reveal more of Gaudí's inventiveness. In the hall, a fireside alcove is scooped out from the wall whilst above it, wall and ceiling merge in an undulating contour.*

CENTRE ABOVE LEFT: *The arches of the Casa Battló dining room recall Gaudí's earlier involvement with Gothic style.*

CENTRE BELOW LEFT: *The roof of Gaudí's Casa Battló whose fantastic forms are in sharp contrast to the conservative lines of the neighbouring building.*

FAR LEFT: *Casa Battló: the sinuous curves continued in the stairwell. The sense of natural forms is increased by the bizarre vertebrae silhouette of the staircase.*

images that impressed itself on Gaudí was that of Montserrat, the mountain behind Barcelona, on which stands a Benedictine monastery dedicated to the Virgin Mary as well as being the legendary resting place of the Holy Grail. Perhaps the completed Sagrada Familia has elements of a holy mountain and a gothicized natural rock formation. Certainly the finished church would have been on a grand scale, what is left today is merely the façade of one transept. In the Sagrada Familia and its encrustations of sculpture, mosaic and glass, one sees Gaudí's obsession, the project that epitomizes all that is unique in his art, and thus a building that defies inclusion in any category whose construction continued long after Art Nouveau had died as a style.

If, in Barcelona, Gaudí provided examples of liberated fantasy at one end of the Art Nouveau spectrum, then at the opposite end of Europe, in Glasgow, Charles Rennie Mackintosh was establishing a style of greater restraint in which free-flowing forms were more carefully controlled. Mackintosh and his wife constituted one half of the Scottish group of designers, 'The Four', who were themselves part of a larger crafts group in Glasgow with strong Art Nouveau connections. However his work as an architect necessarily set him slightly apart from the intricacies of purely decorative art. This more austere art can best be seen in Mackintosh's Glasgow School of Art, which launched his career as an independent architect in 1897. The asymmetry and the hint of turrets evident in the front entrance refer to Mackintosh's early enthusiasm for the Gothic revival. In the starkly-mullioned great windows of the north-facing studies and the apparent simplicity of the whole, there is evidence of the influence of the uniquely British Arts and Crafts architects with their Tudor references. Yet Mackintosh is a figure of European significance for the Art Nouveau, and like Gaudí, his importance extends

beyond the local. Thus, in the curving stonework in the centre of the main façade and the stylized elongation of the windows of the west front display is the refinement of Art Nouveau and the connection becomes stronger in the details of the building. The carving over the entrance has the curving, Celtic lines of Art Nouveau graphics and metalwork of the Glasgow school, and the ironwork indulges in more abstract curves. This is used to contrast with the harder lines of the stone background in a way reminiscent of Horta's Hotel Solvay. The ironwork, resembling buttresses against the main studio window, is rounded off in intricate, loosely-bound knots of metalwork, almost like enlarged pieces of jewellery. The strange decorations on the railings at street level, and the bundles of arrow shapes supporting patterned dishes, derive from Japanese heraldry, stressing the internationalism of Mackintosh's references and his affinity with the orientally-inspired refinements of Art Nouveau.

The simplicity and elegance of Japan are again recalled in the interior of the school's library, designed throughout by Mackintosh. He was reluctant to experiment with structural ironwork, so wood is used throughout to support the galleries. Mackintosh's fascination with beams and joints was a typically eclectic Art Nouveau fusion of his Japanese and Gothic interests, and is seen again in the open rafters elsewhere in the building. The use of dark, stained wood also gives the library interior an oriental sobriety. By opening out a continuous central space, Mackintosh created a slender, vertical beams, echoed in the delicate light fittings, while creating a variation of one of the great themes of Art Nouveau architicture, the open, light and spacious interior, in this case lit by the long, triple bay windows of the west façade.

Mackintosh was a very influential figure in late European Art Nouveau at the beginning of the twentieth century, yet his architectural career is limited largely to the Glasgow School of Art and some houses for private Scottish patrons. His career suffered after a move to England; in order to see the architecture of those who appreciated his work it is necessary to turn to the Austrian Art Nouveau of Vienna.

The Viennese Secession group of artists and architects had been formed in 1897, both as a reaction to the tired revivalism of academic artists and as a celebration of modernity. It was therefore almost inevitable that the work of its members should directly reflect the influence of the Art Nouveau style which by then was fully-developed in Western Europe. The Secession Style, as it was known in Vienna, began as something of a local variant on Art Nouveau. This late flowering of the style was to prove to be a turning point

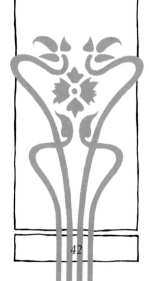

LEFT: *The Casa Milá, with its wrought iron balconies, that recall tangled seaweed.*

between Art Nouveau opulence and 20th century austerity. Even in their earlier works, the Austrian architects preferred a framework of straighter lines to set off the opulent curves of Art Nouveau. They were particularly appreciative of these qualities in Mackintosh's style, which helped to form their own, and of the English Arts and Crafts architects who, by this stage, were opposing the sensuality of Art Nouveau. The master of the older generation was Otto Wagner (1841-1918). An influential writer and theorist. Wagner's architectural career had not brought him a great deal of public success; the Secession supported his pupils, Josef Maria Olbrich and Josef Hoffmann, who were founding members. In 1899, Wagner became a full member of the Secession and severed his connections with his own generation.

The year before, Wagner had publicly shown his allegiance to the Secession style by his treatment of the façade of an apartment block he had designed, aptly dubbed the Majolikahaus. In essence, this consisted of a completely regular grid of windows, devoid of any architectural or sculptural decoration. However, to counteract this austerity Wagner decorated

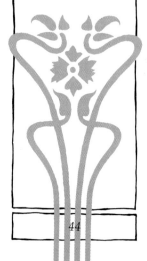

the whole façade with brightly-coloured majolica, floral-patterned tiles that seemed to grow up from the second floor, gradually enveloping the whole building in the light, sinuous lines of Viennese Art Nouveau. It has been suggested that it was his pupil, Olbrich, who was principally responsible for the temporary conversion of Wagner to a local variant of Art Nouveau. Certainly Olbrich's own sympathies were with the more exotic strains that were then in vogue. He was also interested in the contemporary revival of crafts, having travelled to England to study developments there. Olbrich and Hoffmann were later to found the Austrian equivalent of Morris & Co or the Century Guild, the *Wiener Werkstätte* (Vienna Workshop).

Before the establishment of the Secession group, Olbrich was working as Wagner's assistant when the latter was appointed architect to the new Viennese underground and suburban railway, the Stadtbahn. The design of the Stadtbahn stations immediately invite comparison with Guimard's work for the Paris Métro. They lack the free-flowing fantasy of Guimard, yet they have a rather Roccoco grace and lightness, with abundant floral detailing, which is the closest point in Austrian architecture to the French style of Art Nouveau. Olbrich's own contribution to the Secession was designing the group's exhibition building, reputedly inspired by a rough sketch by Gustav Klimt. The central feature of the Secession Building is a hollow dome, framed by four towers, and entirely constructed of metal leaves. This almost matched Gaudí in fantastic invention, but it is telling that the shape of this crowning foliage is a perfect hemisphere, a poised form of rest rather than a restless growth. The details continue the theme of the dome around the main entrance and at either side but the carved foliage, although intricately woven, is restrained by being framed within rectangular panels from which only the occasional, suspended stem is allowed to escape. Like much of the Secession's work in all art forms, the effect is achieved through well-controlled contrast rather

•

LEFT: *The Karlsplatz Station of the Vienna Stadtbahn (subway train) by Wagner.*

CENTRE ABOVE LEFT: *Otto Wagner's Majolica House, showing the combination of severity and ornament typical of the Viennese secession movement.*

CENTRE BELOW LEFT: *Otto Wagner's Post Office Savings Bank, Vienna, a transitional design between Art Nouveau and Art Deco, well in advance of its time.*

FAR LEFT: *Josef Maria Olbrich's Secession building, Vienna whose strong lines are enlivened by the foliage and writhing snakes over the entrance.*

●

ABOVE RIGHT: *In structure, Sullivan's Carson, Pirie Scott department store in Chicago, Illinois anticipates much of 20th century architecture.*

BELOW: *The decorative metalwork over the Carson, Pirie Scott store recalls the florid exuberance of Art Nouveau.*

than an unbridled release of free-flowing form. This is a development of the 'classic' Art Nouveau style into something new, and it was to be the theme of early 20th century architecture, which eventually discarded all non architectural ornament. This is largely true even of Wagner's later work, though his design for the Postsparkasse (Post Office Savings Bank) in Vienna (1904), the openness of the interior, the attention to every detail of furniture and fitting, the light, glass roof and particularly the elegantly tapering piers supporting the gently curved vault, all suggest the remaining echoes of Art Nouveau.

In America, the same contrast between lush ornament and more rigid structure was being explored by Louis Sullivan, the leader of an innovative group of

LEFT: Louis Sullivan's Auditorium Building, whose austere façade contrasts with the lavishness of some of the interior decoration.

architects based in the booming city of Chicago. Sullivan's importance as a pioneer of twentieth century architecture extends beyond the isolated decade or so of Art Nouveau. He led the movement toward exploitation of the new steel-framed structures, which, with the development of the elevator, enabled him to produce the most successful early skyscrapers. His architecture is more concerned with expressing the structural skeleton of the building, by allowing a very plain grid form to appear as the basic design and by hollowing out the ground floor until it rests on just a few reinforced columns. These innovations of Sullivan's were eventually to become commonplace in modern architecture throughout the world.

Yet Sullivan remained very much a man of his time in his attitude toward the embellishment of his buildings. His theories on the subject were highly developed and he saw the contrast between the rectilinear and curvilinear as parallel to the division beween intellect and emotion, and throughout his architecture he tried to maintain a balance between the two. The actual form of his ornament was often reminiscent of oriental abstractions from nature, but just as frequently he used more overt natural forms of intertwining leaves and branches which became very much a Chicago version of Art Nouveau, home-grown but with very strong formal links with the style as it had developed within Europe. The bar interior of the great Auditorium Building, a complex of opera house, hotel and offices, shows an opulence of detail and the involvement of the architect in every small feature, which is wholly characteristic of Art Nouveau. Nor was Sullivan adverse to turning his bare exposed vertical beams, part of his grid façade, into rather exotic tree forms by a flourish of foliage at the top, as in the façade of the Gage Building of South Michigan Avenue, Chicago. More frequently, Sullivan preferred to contain very lush and flowing natural ornament within quite rigid limits, as in the Wainwright Building in St Louis, where it serves to articulate the horizontal beams set against the plain verticals, and to embellish a very ornate cornice which caps the whole composition. The natural forms of Sullivan's decoration not only recalled those of French Art Nouveau, but also had symbolic importance for him. The energy of organic growth was what Sullivan was attempting to evoke, and in particular its application to the rapidly developing cities of America. Just as Art Nouveau was self-consciously the modern style, so Sullivan was attempting to create a powerful, growing architecture.

His Guaranty Building in Buffalo, New York, extends this Art Nouveau concern for growth beyond the decoration itself, into the structure as a whole. Linked by arches at their peak, the great verticals of the building seem to be enormous stems pushing up to the cornice which curls over in a gentle curve reminiscent of growing form. In this case, the ornament makes the analogies more explicit. Sullivan's last great work, the then Carson, Pirie & Scott department store in Chicago, seems for the main area of its façade to be too plain for any reference to Art Nouveau to be made, yet in the first two storeys, and particularly around the corner entrance, there is reliefwork of Gaudí-like extravagance even, in this unlikly context, recalling the Sagrada Familia. This seems largely based on an elaborate Gothic fantasy, yet its tense spider's web lines and twisting foliage can ultimately only be seen as a personal Art Nouveau composition.

FURNITURE

*A desk and chair in Louis Majorelles's later style, showing a
more restrained use of curving forms.*

ART NOUVEAU

●

BELOW RIGHT: A rare use of fantastic grotesques by Gallé. Charactistically, the whole table leg is given over to their form.

Art Nouveau furniture bears all the variety of the regional styles of the movement. True to the spirit of Art Nouveau, few craftsmen specialized exclusively in furniture, and most had been trained in other arts or crafts. Most Art Nouveau furniture makers had been, or remained, architects, concerned to extend their control into the interior of their buildings. The same tensions between ornament and structure, form and function were evident in furniture making as they were in architecture.

Through the range of Art Nouveau furniture it is possible to see designs stripped down to the most elegant bare curves, as well as those which are adorned with carving, brass, gilt or ivory. A similar contrast exists between designs that are obviously designed for comfort and utility, and those that come close to sacrificing both these concerns for the sake of effect. What gives coherence to this variety are the irrepressible curves and sense of idiosyncratic inventiveness. Occasionally these had to be curbed especially when designs were intended for mass production. The attention to detail and the manipulation of the materials generally meant that Art Nouveau furniture was unsuited to any mode of production other than that of the individual craftsman. As in the Arts and Crafts movement in England, the Art Nouveau designer was forced to accept the fact that his work was primarily an expensive luxury for an élite, despite whatever Morris-like Utopian ideals of art for everyone he might hold. Factory-produced Art Nouveau furniture inevitably lost much of its natural vitality and was a coarsened version of the hand-worked equivalent. Art Nouveau architects might have been eager to embrace the new materials of iron and steel, but when they turned to designing furniture their style was fundamentally unsuited to modern production techniques.

Much of the vitality of Art Nouveau derived from various provincial centres. In France, the decorative arts were not confined to Paris, but also flourished in the city of Nancy in Lorraine. Nancy was historically the home of the glass-making industry. The leader of the Art Nouveau revival of Nancy's main industry was Emil Gallé (1846-1904),heir to a small ceramic and glassware business. Gallé travelled to England in the 1870s and had been caught up in the growing enthusiasm for the decorative arts. He also studied the oriental art collection of the Victoria and Albert Museum in London and, with his new found knowledge of Chinese and Japanese techniques, he returned to Nancy to revitalize his father's workshop. Gallé was not only an enthusiastic orientalist but also possessed a specialist's knowledge of botany and entomology, his other amateur passions. He was equipped with a very detailed first-hand knowledge of leaf, flower and insect forms, which, when combined with the decorative, abstract tendency of the Japanese, combined to form the Art Nouveau blend. A third ingredient, rococo, was already evident in Nancy, which had many fine houses and decorations in that style.

In 1884, after some years of working in glass and ceramics, Gallé started designing and producing furniture. At first his designs were somewhat ponderous though but invariably enlivened with vivid natural details. Success came at the 1889 Paris International Exhibition, where Gallé was acknowledged as an innovator, creating a new style in reaction to the unimaginative revivalism of contemporary French furniture. Gallé's work became increasingly lighter and more ornate. Natural forms were not restricted to detail; whole arms, legs and backs were carved in plant or insect forms, curving and twisting to animate the whole and seeming to defy the nature of the wood itself. Although stylized, those graceful shapes were always clearly identifiable plants of a species known to Gallé. His favourites were local plants including cow-parsley, water lilies, orchids and irises though he also used exotics, such as bamboo.

Gallé preferred soft woods, of which he had a very thorough knowledge, to facilitate the creation of his effects, which included his remarkable revival of the art of marquetry. Most of the surfaces of Gallé's furniture became fields for the most intricate inlays featuring plants, insects or landscapes in what could

51

BELOW RIGHT: *Mantelpiece by|Eugène Vallin. The designer worked with a greater feeling for sculptural form than his master, Gallé.*

become an overloading of effects. So fine was the craftsmanship, though, that Gallé's own willowy signature could be reproduced on his pieces.

Gallé's mastery of marquetry opened the way to the expression of poetry and literary themes in his furniture. He liked to include suitable quotations and, as a mark of the fusion of arts and crafts in Art Nouveau, he gave some pieces names in the manner of paintings or music. A console he created became *Les Parfums d'Autrefois* (Perfumes of the Past) and his last masterpiece, the bed he designed while dying of leukemia, *Aube et Crépuscule* (Dawn and Dusk). This latter piece is evidence of Gallé's increasing restraint in his late style, simplifying forms and eradicating much of the over-intricacy of his earlier work, as well as being a tour-de-force of marquetry. The dark shadows of dusk are enveloped in the drooping wings of a fantastic insect on the headboard, while at the foot of the bed

the rising wings of another huge insect are depicted in lighter woods and mother-of-pearl.

Gallé was the inspiration behind a couple of craftsmen, termed the Nancy School, who became a loosely formal group in 1901 with the foundation of the Alliance Provinciale des Industries d'Art (1859-1926). Second to Gallé was Louis Majorelle who trained as a painter but then concentrated on running his family's furniture business in Nancy. Majorelle began designing in an 18th-century style until persuaded by Gallé to inject a more vital naturalism into his work His pieces are, nevertheless, rather more solid than Gallé's, partly because he favoured the use of harder, more exotic woods. The more sculptural elements in Majorelle's pieces come in the ornamentation, which, still partly inspired by the baroque and rococo, he added in gilt, copper or bronze. Majorelle equalled Gallé in the quality of his marquetry, but generally his

style differs in its smoother lines. Majorelle was consequently able to make a successful transition to the simpler style of the 1920s.

Other cabinetmakers in Nancy worked for either Majorelle or Gallé, and occasionally both. Victor Prouvé (1858-1943) specialized in marquetry work for both masters as well as designing his own pieces. Eugène Vallin (1856-1925) worked for Gallé and produced pieces of a far greater weight than those of his master. Vallin's work eschews intricate natural detail and instead concentrates on broad, swaying, linear rhythms anticipating the end of his career when he took up architecture and used cast concrete for his effects. Jacques Gruber produced designs for Majorelle and was also Professor of Decorative Arts at the Ecole des Beaux-Arts in Nancy. His furniture shares the same flowing forms as that of Vallin, and is removed from Gallé's roccoco touches.

●

RIGHT: *Room setting of furniture by the Parisian designer Georges Hoentschel. Furniture, as any product of Art Nouveau, was designed to be seen as part of a unified environment.*

In Paris, Samuel Bing's 'Galerie de l'Art Nouveau' was the principal showcase for Art Nouveau furniture, as for other crafts. Reflecting the nationalism fashionable in time in France at the time, Bing encouraged the craftsmen who worked for him to study the great French tradition of 'grace, elegance, purity and sound logic', and principally the refined poise of 18th-century work. The Parisian Art Nouveau designers tended to avoid the more overtly floral detailing of Nancy and concentrated instead on a purity of light, flowing line. Bing showed a great range of work, but he favoured a nucleus of three furniture makers: Eugène Gaillard, Georges de Feure and Edward Colonna.

Gaillard represents the functional side of Art Nouveau furniture; he studied the problem of function in design and produced designs of an increasingly light, almost classic, simplicity. His chairs were concerned with comfort, had moulded backs, sometimes padding at the shoulder, and leather or fabric-covered coil-sprung, upholstered seats. Georges de Feure, a painter

and poet, was something of a dandy. He was a keeper of greyhounds, which he admired for their fine Art Nouveau lines. He brought more colour and decoration to his furniture, with gilding and coloured lacqueur, as well as the kind of carved detail rare in Gaillard's work. The third, Edward Eugène Colonna, had emigrated from Cologne to America where he worked under Tiffany, before returning to Europe to continue his carrer in Paris, Colonna's furniture, like de Feure's was part of a larger output including procelain and fabrics, and had a delicate, attenuated elegance also close to de Feure's style. When Bing was honoured with his own pavilion devoted to Art Nouveau at the 1900 Paris World's Fair, these three designers were given the task of decorating and furnishing it.

In England, the major crafts began to veer away from the Art Nouveau style at the beginnning of the twentieth century. This was paradoxical as Mackmurdo and his Century Guild had virtually created it in the 1880s. At that time Mackmurdo had produced

LEFT: *Office suite, consisting of a desk, matching chair and sideboard by Eugène Vallin, in the exaggerated Art Nouveau style, known in France as* Style Liberty.

BELOW LEFT: *Chair by Gaillard. The leather upholstery and simple lines show a concern for function above uncontrolled fantasy.*

some furniture with carving that used the unmistakable swirling forms of his frontispiece to *Wren's City Churches,* but by the time the style was common elsewhere, English designers had retreated to harder rectilinear forms or the simplicity of cottage styles. The same was largely true in the United States, where the influence of the English Arts and Crafts work, and a national preference for a simple Gothic style, was strong, However, the exception was the American designer Charles Rohlfs, who was very successful. Rohlfs retired from an acting career to concentrate upon crafts, and managed to skillfully combine the swirling forms of European Art Nouveau with the native influence of the Baroque-inspired Mission style, giving his furniture a cosmopolitan aura flavoured with an individually native touch. Rohlfs exhibited at Turin in 1902 and was successful enough to open eight showrooms in the United States, with headquarters in Buffalo.

ABOVE LEFT: *The Art Nouveau curve of the legs of this table by Edward Colonna is underplayed in its refinement, and emphasizes the stylistic differences between Bing's Parisian designers and the more exaberant work of their counterparts in Nancy.*

BELOW LEFT: *Occasional table by Hector Guimard, showing the same rather taught, sinuous shapes as his entrances for the Paris Métro.*

OPPOSITE ABOVE LEFT: *American furniture by Solomon Karpen Bros of Chicago. Curves, natural ornament and the long-tressed Art Nouveau maiden are all prominent, but a stolid heaviness still prevails.*

OPPOSITE CENTRE LEFT: *An elegant screen by de Feure.*

OPPOSITE BELOW LEFT: *Chair by Josef Hoffman, leader of the Viennese Secession.*

CENTRE: *A console table by Georges de Feure. The forms are pure Art Nouveau but the gilding reveals 18th century inspiration.*

MACKINTOSH

England was unresponsive to the Art Nouveau style in furniture, but Britain as a whole was represented by Scottish designers, and in particular the Glasgow school. In furniture, as in architecture, it was Mackintosh's work that dominated. Mackintosh's furniture, is intended to be seen as part of a whole interior design with secondary work often designed by other members of The Four, and as such has many similarities with his architecture. In England, Mackintosh's designs were regarded with suspicion for being too stylized, or 'aesthetic', and certainly his furniture is created more for an aesthetic effect than for either comfort or to display the natural quality of the materials. As in his architecture, Mackintosh concentrated

FAR LEFT: *Black chair by Charles Rennie Mackintosh. Mackintosh was reluctant to incorporate natural wood grain into his design.*

LEFT: *Charles Rennie Mackintosh's furniture in the board room of the Glasgow School of Art. A simple, strong contrast of black and white in a Japanese vein was the keystone of much of Mackintosh's design.*

ABOVE: *An ebonised Charles Rennie Mackintosh cabinet with panels painted by his wife Margaret Macdonald.*

BELOW: *White-painted table by Charles Rennie Mackintosh.*

upon extremely elegant, exaggerated verticals, particularly in the backs of his chairs which could be exceptionally tall and slender. These were cut into ovals, grids or ladderbacks that descended down to the floor. Curves might occur, but with Mackintosh they were primarily used to stress the rigidity of verticals. A Japanese simplicity reveals itself occasionally, as in the domino table for the Ingram Street Tea Room, where sections seem almost to be slotted together by simple joinery. Mackintosh felt uncomfortable with the natural grain of the wood and attempted to minimalize it by deep, dark staining and eventually by lacquering or ebonizing it into matt black. He explored a converse neutrality by painting other pieces white to act as a suitable background for lilac and silver harmonies. On lighter furniture, Mackintosh stencilled stylized designs.

●

Chairs by Koloman Moser of the Viennese Secession movement, showing the great restraint of the style partly inspired by Mackintosh.

BELOW RIGHT: *Cabinet and chair by the Viennese Secessionist Josef Maria Olbrich.*

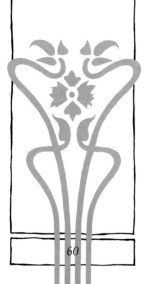

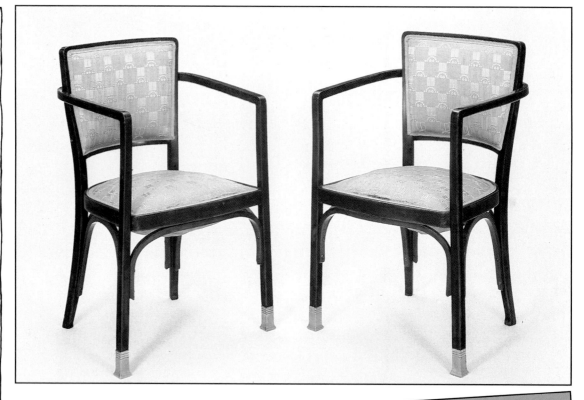

Mackintosh's influence emerged most strongly in Vienna with the artists of the Secession movement. In 1903, the Secession moved into crafts, including furniture designs with the foundation of the Wiener Werkstätte, a Viennese arts and crafts guild, headed by the architect Josef Hoffmann and the painter Koloman Moser. Wiener Werkstätte furniture has the luxury of materials — rich veneers, marquetry and gilding — associated with Art Nouveau and the Secession Style (*Secezionstil*), but is rigid angularity is a continuation of Mackintosh's style that places it in the concluding chapter of a discussion of Art Nouveau. Similarly elusive of categorization is the furniture of the extraordinary Italian designer, Carlo Bugatti, which was the sensation and *cause célèbre* of the Turin Exhibition in 1902. Bugatti represents the culmination of the nineteenth-century fascination for the exotic, in his case a Moorish, Egyptian and Byzantine fantasy. Almost every material was used to enhance these references in his furniture: carved and painted wood, polished brass and copper, painted vellum and rich silks. The overall effect is certainly powerful. To some it was magnificently theatrical, to others pompous and coarse. The ornateness, the unity of theme, and the use of broad, sweeping arcs all relate Bugatti to Art Nouveau, but there is much, too, that sets him apart from all contemporaries and places him as a pioneer of Art Deco and Hollywood glamour.

CHAPTER FOUR

METALWORK

*Teaset by Archibald Knox for Liberty & Co, part of the Tudric
range he designed continuing the Celtic theme.*

RIGHT: The gate of Horta's Van Eetvelde House introduces the style that is to reappear in the ironwork bannisters of the interior.

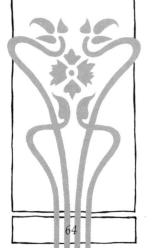

Wrought-iron has already been seen as a significant part of Art Nouveau architecture, both structurally and decoratively. Victor Horta had made its structural use clear in his work in Brussels and he had also used it decoratively, exploiting its relative malleability to provide lighter patterns in contrast to the weightiness of stone. In Art Nouveau architecture, metalwork serves as a link between the building itself and the style of its contents, often the product of the same designer. From exterior balconies, gates and window mullions it continues to the interior in columns, beams, bannisters and door handles, and even to embellishments on furniture, With metalwork, the versatility of use and range of metals available meant that almost every Art Nouveau interior designer turned his hand to metalwork at some stage. Like many another Art Nouveau medium, it is important to visualize metalwork as part of its context in the interior. It could appear in the form of candlesticks, candelabra, cutlery, clocks, light fittings, mirrors, tableware, caskets or combs.

Guimard's Métro entrances emphasize the versatility of the medium as they can be seen as architecture as well as architectural sculpture or even enormous decorative pieces. They use the same forms as his great iron gates for the Castel Béranger apartments as well as the bannisters within. Horta carried the same continuity of form from the iron balconies to the bannisters for the staircase, the main architectural and sculptural feature of the interior of his magnificent home in the Rue Americaine in Brussels,as well

as in the other homes he designed. Comparable in function, although more fantastic in form, were the balconies of Gaudí's Casa Milá, modelled like tangled masses of seaweed. It is easier to separate Gaudí the metalworker from Gaudí the architect, since he executed metalwork at times independent of his buildings and as a composition in its own right. Gaudí's father had been a coppersmith, and he must have been profoundly influenced by seeing this malleable material being worked at heat. Certainly Gaudí treated wrought iron as if it were as tractable, particularly in the form of grilles and gates. In his early work for the Casa Vicens he achieved the effect of palm fronds with the spikes cut at the top bent in every direction as if they were drooping leaves. His entrance gate to the Güell Estate in Pedralbes is even more oustanding, for almost the entire piece is given the form of a writhing dragon whose gaping jaws reach out for the visitor as he grasps the handle. Such a bizarre fantasy is more easily absorbed in the small-scale medium of jewellery; to see it on such a large scale is shocking. The gate was produced in 1885 and reveals that Gaudí had already reached the peak of Art Nouveau sinuous form and fantasy in metalwork when his architecture was still in the Gothic style.

Work in the more traditional precious metals, particularly silver, had sunk to a low level of design and workmanship through industrialization until it was revived by the English Arts and Crafts movement. These craftsmen stressed the virtues of hand-made objects, and even occasionally chose to stress the method of production with obviously hand-produced hammered dents left on the surface. Less precious metals were often also used for cutlery (flatware) which was normally associated with silver. Knives, forks and spoons might be made of bronze, brass, tin, pewter or copper, which were often easier to use for more daring designers. As well as having fewer of the historical associations of the more traditional materials, they could be more readily associated with a new style linked to political convictions and beliefs. Art Nouveau crftsmen liked to work across the complete range of metals, at times mixing them with enamel,ivory, wood or anything other material required to create the appropriate effect.

A typical Art Nouveau duality appeared with regards to the means of production. Some designers, following in the Arts and Crafts wake, produced hand-made and therefore very exclusive items, while others tailored their designs to large-scale production and found themselves more in tune with the future course of design. The work of The Four, the Glasgow group around Mackintosh, falls into the former category.

●

LEFT: *The elaborately-treated iron balconies and columns on the façade of Horta's house.*

ABOVE RIGHT: Silver biscuit (cookie) box by Archibald Knox with decorations deriving from Celtic and Nordic interlacing patterns.

BELOW RIGHT: Another Knox teaset for Liberty and Co. with echoes of Art Nouveau in the elongated forms and asymetrical settings of the enamel ornament.

Half of the Four, the sisters Margaret and Frances Macdonald (the former being Mrs Mackintosh), produced together and singly much relief work, either of beaten tin or silver, as mounts for objects such as mirrors or as decorative objects in their own right. The pale coolness of these pieces perfectly complement the Mackintosh interior and add a figurative and floral dimension to the Glasgow style. Elongated, undulating maidens derived from Toorop are a common feature, as well as rather spikey growths whose long tendrils weave themselves into Celtic patterns or droop into Art Nouveau curves. A hand-crafted impression is created by the frequent use of a rough ground to offset the more polished figures.

A similar mood is created in the metalwork of Alexander Knox, the principal designer for the Liberty department store in London, who had actually studied Celtic design in the appropriate setting of Douglas School of Art on the Isle of Man. Knox worked more exclusively with silver, often setting it with semi-precious stones to produce exquisitely-designed work decorated with sparsely-applied Celtic-style relief. These works were produced in some quantity for the store, as were the designs of Christopher Dresser.

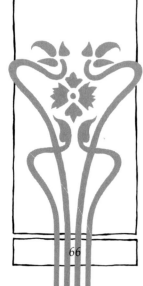

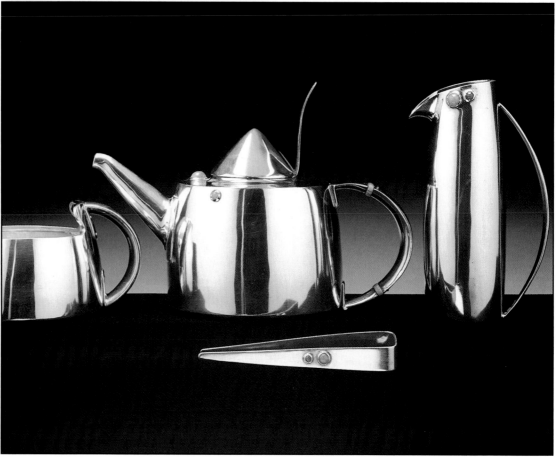

ABOVE RIGHT: *Copper wall sconce by the Glasgow designer Marian Wilson, which combines a smoothly-finished motif with an obviously handworked ground.*

BELOW RIGHT: *Teaset of oriental refinement by Christopher Dresser.*

Dresser was one of the few craftsmen of the time to have visited Japan, as evidenced by the restrained purity of line in his work. Only rarely does a sweeping curve of Art Nouveau appear, since Dresser was more concerned with function and economy to simplify the mass-production process. In Germany, factories had managed to a surprising degree to combine large-scale production with some of the most extravagant Art Nouveau pieces of tableware. This was particularly true of the products of the Württembürgische Metallwarenfabrik (WMF) works at Geislingen, although the Metallenfabrik Eduard Hueck at Ludenschied also produced designs by such leading figures as Behrens and Olbrich.

In France the Nancy school concentrated more on furniture, glass and ceramics, although Louis Majorelle, who had used gilt trimmings on his furniture, produced some gates and bannisters as did Victor Prouvé. More metalwork was produced by the Parisian craftsmen working for Bing and Meier-Graefe. The elegant Georges de Feure was one of the most versatile of these and designed objects, from candelabra to cane handles, based on stylized, fluid, plant forms. Others, like Colonna or Selmersheim turned to metalwork for a complete room setting, designing table-lamps, or chandeliers in the form of drooping plants whose flowers were the glass shades. Lucien Gaillard, who took over the family metalwork business in 1892, produced work of outright fantasy with intricate high relief detailing of grasshoppers, stag-beetles or vines. This sort of very naturalistic detail, surrealistically clustering on an everyday object, suggests the role of jewellery on a dress. In 1900, encouraged by René Lalique, Gaillard explored the possibilities of

copper and bronze, as did Guimard, in a number of vases whose necks are twisted into an intertwining, restless abstract surface of strands.

The use of the human figure in Art Nouveau metalwork clearly draws it closer to sculpture. The bronze reliefs by Alexandre Charpentier of nude women in undulating poses set against the background of their impossibly long, flowing hair, seem to straddle the gap between art and craft, only the inconsequentiality of their subject matter drawing them back toward the latter. French sculpture at the time was dominated by the ageing giant, Auguste Rodin, whose work, principally in bronze, had exploited to the full that medium's possibilities for active poses and shimmering light. Rodin's work is too involved with symbolist and literary overtones to be described as decorative, yet his frequently twisting poses and erotic subjects recall some aspects of Art Nouveau. Certainly the flowing

relief of his *Gates of Hell* recalls the forms of subsequent, decorative Art Nouveau reliefs, such as the abstract patterning of Guimard's vestibule to the Castel Béranger. Similar, yet tiny, flowing groups of figures appear carved from ivory on a vase and a brooch by Lalique and have been attributed to Rodin.

The British sculptor Sir Alfred Gilbert, the creator of the Shaftesbury Memorial fountain at Piccadilly Circus in London (better known as 'Eros'), was a sculptor in bronze who made the transition to working on a smaller scale with precious and semi-precious materials. Even in the detailing of his larger public work Gilbert was fascinated by the intricate, grotesque curving and twisting forms, often tinged with elements of marine mythology taken from the 16th and 17th centuries.

Elements later explored in Art Nouveau metalwork had therefore made an earlier appearance in fine art

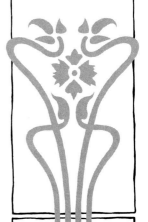

sculpture. The link was maintained by the Art Nouveau vogue for decorative bronze or gilt bronze statuettes, which, like Charpentier's reliefs, were on the borderline between sculpture and jewellery. Many Art Nouveau designers had been trained as sculptors so the connection is clear, yet many of these figures retain a functional side, often as lamps, or, less frequently, as card holders or vases. This was principally a French-inspired fashion pursued by such figures as Eugène Feuillâtre, Raoul Larche, Théodore Rivière and Rupert Carabin, who produced figures of a Gallic gaiety and charm. They were all nude or lightly-draped female figures, often dancers, creating sinuous Art Nouveau arabesques with their flowing hair or drapery. Occasionally, they attempted a more poetic mood in allegorical figures, nymphs, or the typically Art Nouveau hybrid figures of plant-women, metamorphizing into stems and flowers. A more thoughtful note was often struck by busts of maidens with downcast eyes. A regional variant of this genre was pioneered in Belgium by the jeweller Philippe Wolfers, who, in 1904 devoted himself entirely to this form of decorative sculpture. His mixed media figures were characterized by the use of ivory for the flesh. The ivory came from the recently-acquired Belgian Congo, and, for economic reasons, its use was sufficiently encouraged by King Leopold II to provoke a small school of artists following Wolfers in this type of work.

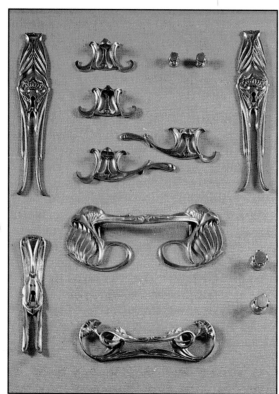

●

LEFT: *A coatstand by the Belgian designer Gustave Serurier-Borry marks the transitional phase of late Art Nouveau when its elongated forms become straighter and less ornate.*

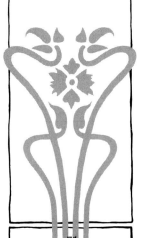

●

ABOVE RIGHT: *Coffee set by Josef Hoffmann, showing the use of scalloped forms and a more typically 18th century mood.*

BELOW RIGHT: *The sinuous, long-haired, lightly-draped Art Nouveau female as she appears on a range of factory produced items.*

BELOW RIGHT: *Sinuous Art Nouveau plants in a silver bowl by C.R. Ashbee of the Guild of Handicrafts. Despite his Arts & Crafts background, Ashbee indulges in a magnificent Art Nouveau flourish in the handles of this piece.*

OPPOSITE LEFT: *A silver bowl by C.R. Ashbee of the Guild of Handicrafts*

OPPOSITE FAR RIGHT: Comedy and Tragedy *by Sir Alfred Gilbert. The fluid grace of the figure connects it with the decorative elements of Art Nouveau.*

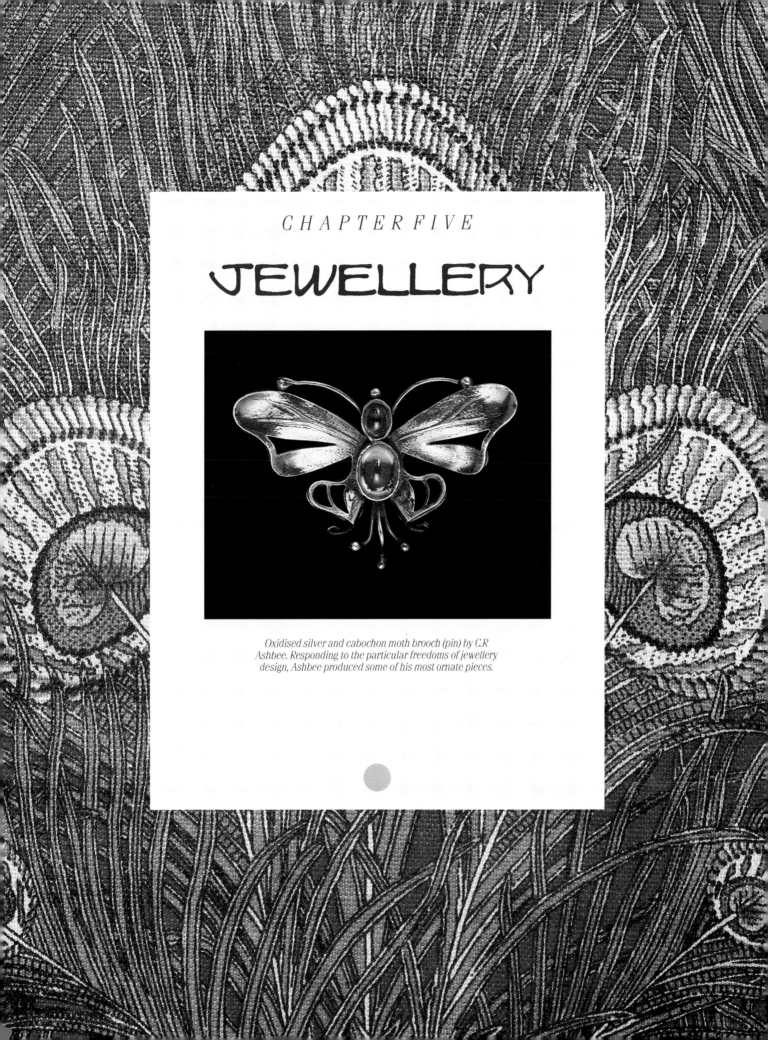

CHAPTER FIVE

JEWELLERY

Oxidised silver and cabochon moth brooch (pin) by C.R Ashbee. Responding to the particular freedoms of jewellery design, Ashbee produced some of his most ornate pieces.

A Lalique clasp in gold-and-enamel, based on a pattern of pine cones and needles.

The great revolutionary designer of Art Nouveau jewellery was the Frenchman René Lalique. Lalique's background was a perfect mixture of art and craft, for on the death of his father he became an apprentice to a goldsmith at the age of 16 while simultaneously studying at the Ecole des Beaux-Arts. He freelanced as a jewellery designer for the Cartier house before becoming an employee of Déstape. In 1886 Déstape handed over the control of his workshop to Lalique in recognition of a unique talent. Lalique's jewellery was first exhibited at the Paris Salon in 1894, and three years later he was awarded the Legion of Honour for his work.

Before Lalique's début, French jewellery was as much concerned with displaying wealth as with art. Precious stones, particularly the cutting and setting of diamonds, had been the focus of the craftsman's skill. There was, in effect, a hierarchy of possible materials that could be used which corresponded entirely to their value and rarity. Strings of glittering stones were undoubtedly prestigious for their wearers but provided little opportunity for the jeweller to stretch his creative powers. Lalique's jewellery was completely uninhibited by such social conventions, and broke with all the traditional rules of design. The result was pieces that were conceived as independent works of art rather than mere ornaments, and Lalique was willing to use any sort of material that was needed to produce his effect. He used semi-precious stones, not as cheap substitutes, but for the sake of their colour, veins or surface. However, in Lalique's work the stones are only a part of the composition as a whole. All types of metal are used as well as onyx, crystal, enamel, glass, mother-of-pearl, amber, ivory and even horn, the latter carved for the first time in jewellery by Lalique. With this far wider range of materials Lalique was able to produce work of an enormous variety of shape and colour, virtually anything that his fantasy suggested. Although the cost of the materials varied the extraordinarily high standard of craftsmanship did not and these extremely intricate creations were thus prized as much for their originality, wit and inventiveness as for their intrinsic value. Some of Lalique's pieces, and those of his comtemporaries, were exotic and striking enough to present a challenge to their wearer's personality. Art Nouveau jewellery was less popular with the middle-classes than with the aristocrats and with actresses. The leading actress of the day was Sarah Bernhardt, who frequently indulged her passion for jewellery by commissioning a piece from Lalique, often for a specific stage role. Apart from aristocrats, actresses and many demi-

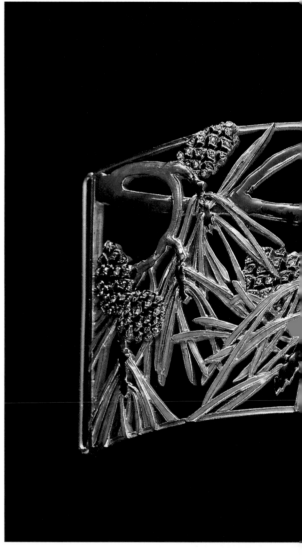

mondaines, Lalique's work was particularly prized by aesthetes, such as the great dandy the Count de Montesquiou. In his vocabulary of natural forms — butterflies, dragonflies, hornets, peacocks, snakes, lilies, orchids and so on — Lalique was the epitome of the Art Nouveau craftsman in any medium, but his eye for anecdote, and particularly his increasing taste for the grotesque and bizarre, brought him closer than many of his contemporaries to the style and concerns of the writers of the day. This was commonly acknowledged by the time of the 1900 Exposition Universelle when Lalique displayed work concerned more than ever with fantastic, even mythological; some, like Medusa, were recognizably literary in their source. Lalique was an excellent draughtsman and conceived his designs as graphic creations; in some ways his jewellery is allied to contemporary illustration. The anecdotal, even narrative, nature of the jewellery was further

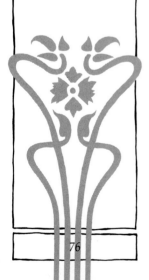

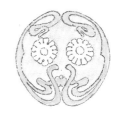

emphasized by Lalique's use of the human figure; neglected by jewellers since the Renaissance, it was resurrected in the Art Nouveau nymph or femme fatale with her long flowing hair and voluptuous figure. The nymph was favoured by the great poets Baudelaire and Mallarmé, whose love of the sinister and erotic also found parallels in Lalique's work. Indeed it has often been remarked that the literary style of the fin-de-siècle 'decadents' strove to emulate jewellery in its fantasy, intricacy, hardness of surface and glittering ornaments.

Lalique's inventiveness, use of materials and supremely high level of craftsmanship made jewellery one of the leading media of Art Nouveau. His work revealed the great potential of jewellery as an art form and inspired a school of imitators in turn-of-the-century Paris. Some were Bing's versatile designers exploring a new form — Colonna and Grasset — yet more were specialists. The Vever brothers, Paul and Henri, turned their family business over to the Lalique style, and specialized in enamel work, as too did Eugène Feuillâtre, who had been trained by Lalique, particularly in three-dimensional enamel work. In 1900, Lalique persuaded his friend, the metalworker Lucien Gaillard, to concentrate his fantasies into the smaller scale of jewellery. Other well-established firms began employing Art Nouveau designers: Lucien Lévy-Dhurmer worked for André Falize, Lucien Bonvallet for Ernest Cardeilhac, while Georges Fouquet employed the great Czech poster designer, Alphonse Mucha, to supply him with designs that rivalled Lalique's for bizarre inventiveness. Mucha was another great favourite of Sarah Bernhardt's, and he designed the posters for her productions as well as supplying her with stage jewellery.

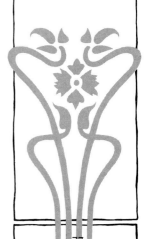

●

RIGHT: *A selection of Art Nouveau jewellery set against a School of Nancy marquetry landscape. The two larger pieces to the left — a hairslide and a parure de corsage — are by Lalique. Evident throughout is the range of colours and materials taking the form of plants or insects.*

●

RIGHT: *A trio including a ring by Archibald Knox and below a gilt-and-lustre Lalique brooch (pin). The bat, with its curving, intricate wings was almost as popular as the dragonfly in Art Nouveau.*

The work of the Parisian jewellers set the fashion for the rest of Europe. In Belgium, Philippe Wolfers produced work in a similar vein until he turned to decorative sculpture in 1904. In America, too, Lalique's influence was felt. Louis Tiffany of Tiffany & Co, already producing Art Nouveau silver, glass and ceramics, set up a jewellery department, under the supervision of the designer, Julia Munson. Even in England, where the Arts and Crafts movement generally shunned what was seen as the florid excess of French Art Nouveau, one of its leading figures, Charles Robert Ashbee, a founder of the Guild of Handicrafts, was seemingly seduced from the simplicity of his style by the decorative possibilities of jewellery. The Arts and Crafts movement and Art Nouveau are at their closest in Ashbee's jewellery which has a flowing, rather Celtic, line. Art Nouveau influence is evident, although Ashbee's materials do not match Lalique's for colour and texture. Characteristic of Ashbee is the use of decorative open wirework, a feature also evident, although reinterpreted in style, in the jewellery of the Glasgow Four. This plainer, more austere, English style can be seen in some of the work of the Belgian van de Velde and the Austro-German school, particularly among the Anglophile craftsmen of the Wiener Werkstätte.

LEFT: *A brooch (pin) by Georges Fouquet.*

RIGHT: *A delicately-enamelled dragonfly hairpiece by Lalique set against a pendant by Philippe Wolfers.*

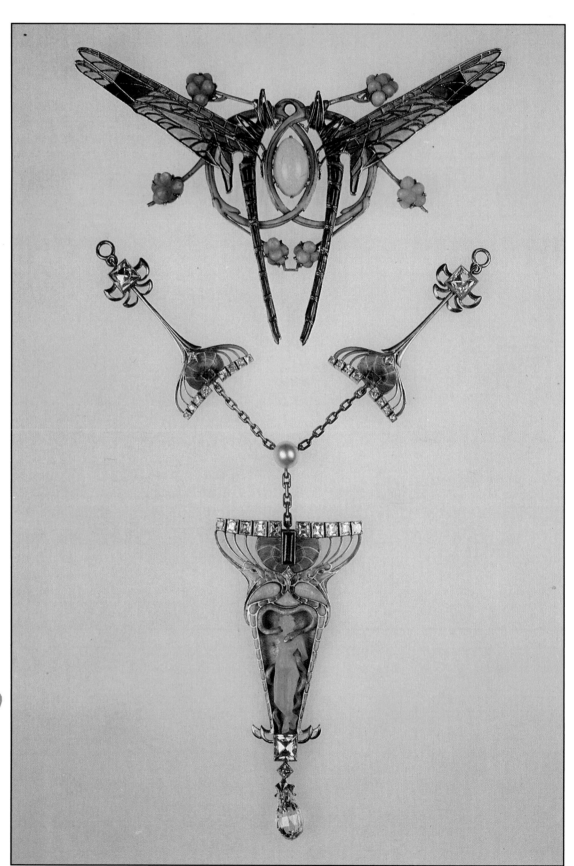

●

LEFT: *Horn and gold hair comb by Georges Fouquet.*

BELOW: *Silver, opal and mother-of-pearl peacock brooch (pin), by C.R. Ashbee.*

CHAPTER SIX

GLASS

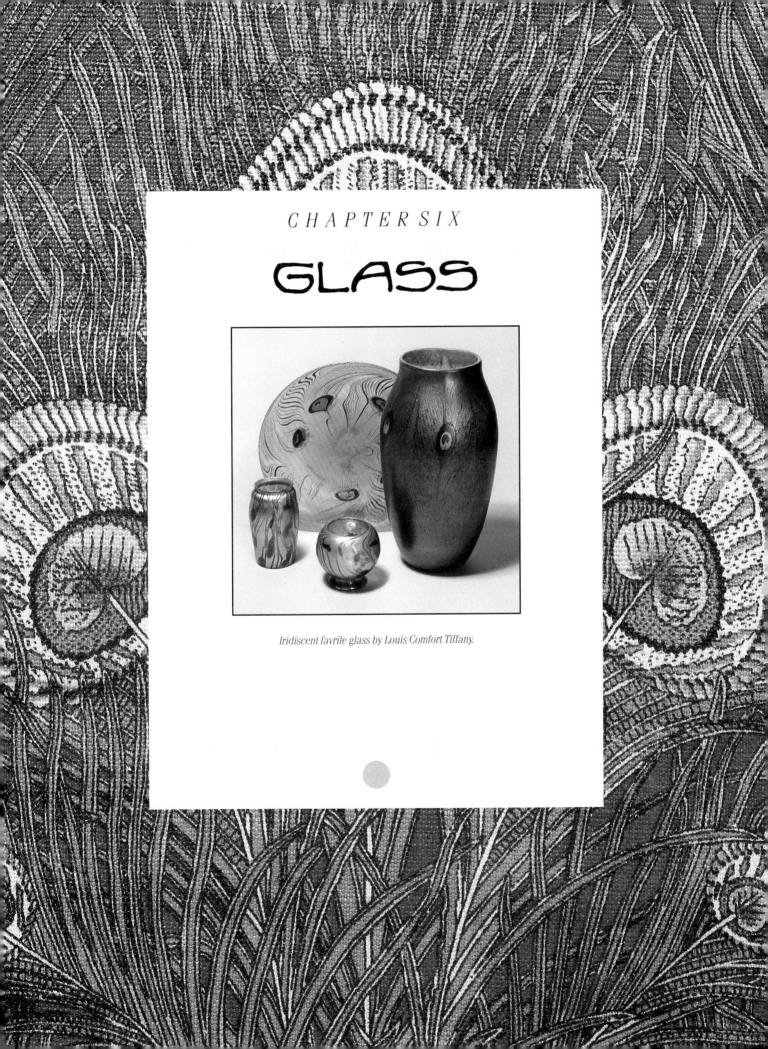

Iridiscent favrile glass by Louis Comfort Tiffany.

For the Art Nouveau craftsman, glass was, in its own way, as malleable and tractable as metal. The fluid contour of Art Nouveau could be as well expressed in the silhouette of a glass vase as in one of silver or bronze, but the translucency of glass was particularly suited to a style that was largely concerned with lightness and delicacy. The Art Nouveau interior presented a theme of openness and airiness, uncluttered and full of light. Glassware continued this theme, for it was the lightest and least substantial medium for the craftsman. Moreover, like stained glass, it could control the tonality and hue of the whole interior if it were set into a window, or the corner of a room if it were used as a lampshade. The designer could paint an interior with the delicacy of a watercolourist through his skill in manipulating the colour effects of glass.

As with the other crafts revitalized by the Art Nouveau, the history of glassware in the earlier 19th century was the story of technical advances, resulting in an impressively consistent quality of mechanical production. This was achieved largely at the expense of the aesthetic distinction created by the hand of the individual craftsman. In England, Morris and his followers had been the first to redress this imbalance in most of the crafts, but glassware was not one of them. To the Arts and Crafts movement glass meant, above all, the stained glass of their neo-medieval church windows. It was not until the 1890s, when Christopher Dresser began designing for the Clutha range of James Couper & Sons of Glasgow, that distinguished contemporary glassware was seen in Britain.

Dresser's electroplate and silverware is strictly and plainly functional in its design, but his work in glass is more flowing and graceful, with an Art Nouveau sense of line and colour.

The great innovators of Art Nouveau glass were French and American. The first was Joseph Brocard who studied Islamic art and restored Arab artefacts in order to learn more about the way they had been made. He was particularly interested in the colour effects that the Islamic craftsmen brought to their glassware through their use of coloured enamel finishes. Brocard's line of thought was followed and developed to its utmost by a series of brilliant technical innovations by Emile Gallé, the greatest master of Art Nouveau glassware.

Although producing furniture, ceramics, metalwork and textiles the Nancy School and Gallé as its chief designer, based its reputation upon the production of Art Nouveau glassware, glass being the traditional industry of the city. Gallé inherited his father's glass decorating workshop and, apart from his botanic and literary studies, his education included a year at the Meisenthal glassworks (now in Germany) which encouraged him to open his own glassworks in 1874. The inspiration for Gallé's work as a designer came partly from his great knowledge of botany and natural history, and, partly from his study of oriental glass and china, which began in London. Although the motto over his workshop door was 'My roots are deep in the woods', it was his study of the techniques of Japanese and Chinese glassmaking that helped him to give form to his delicate and tender vision of the natural world. Two of his great innovations were unveiled at the Parisian World Exhibitions of 1878 and 1889. Both his 'clair de lune' glass with its delicate sapphire tinge, and his relief moulded cameo glass were ultimately based on oriental techniques, Japanese and Chinese respectively.

Gallé increasing came to realize the full potential of glass as a medium. He began to explore the possibilities of colour, at first translucent, as in the 'clair de lune' work and then, in 1889, opaque colour, which made a greater range possible. Degrees of colour and translucency could be controlled by varying the process employed, and beautifully subtle light effects could be produced, evoking water or the atmosphere. Many more surface effects could be obtained by experimenting with the oxidation of the piece by acid baths, or using acid in the engraving process.

Gallé began to achieve relief effects by moulding the glass, adding further coatings or by using acid to strip down layers. Combined with effects of colour and translucence, this could provide marvellous effects of

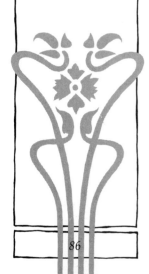

BELOW RIGHT: *An early ewer by Gallé, influenced by the rococo, and a later bowl. The latter shows a more highly developed sense of relief, and more active form.*

BELOW FAR RIGHT: *A Gallé vase that reproduces the green and blue tints of underwater plant life beneath a relief detail of the plants themselves.*

underwater creatures against drifting waterweed, beetles crawling through the long grass or a butterfly alighting on a high branch. Gallé could also experiment by embedding further elements within the glass itself, such as metal leaf, gold dust or enamel, similar to the way in which an oil painter builds up his painting through the accumulation of subtly tinted, translucent layers of paint. The control of every technical detail of temperature and chemical mixtures had to be precise for a successful result. Gallé's mastery was such that he could exploit the production process to enhance the appearance of the piece, as in the careful creation of deliberate crazing in quartz to produce delicate, coloured veins as a feature, rather than a flaw. A combination of different ingredients might also be used, as in the *champlevé* technique in which cavities created in the glass were lined with gilt before being filled in by layers of translucent enamel whose glow would be enhanced by their backing. The use of enamel combined with glass gave Gallé the scope for deeper and more diverse colour, while the technique of *marquetrie-sur-verre*, the blending of semi-molten layers of glass on a semi-molten body, gave him a sculptor's control of form.

Glass was Gallé's natural medium. That which might appear florid and overwrought in his furniture became delicate and ethereal in his glassware. Gallé's nature studies were at their best in glasses, beakers and vases, since they allowed him to create a micro-cosm of the real world, where an insect's wing or a petal could be the largest form of the composition. Gallé's creation of beauty, mystery and surprise from what in natural or botanic terms was often mundane, was truly poetic. In the best Art Nouveau tradition, his glassware was prized far more as an artistic creation than for its functional design, and it was collected by writers and aesthetes. The admiration was mutual, for Gallé found much inspiration in poetry's celebration of exquisite sensation. He created his *verreries parlantes*- talking glassware — as a tribute to literature. Glassware inscribed with quotes from his favourite writers — Mallarmé, Rimbaud, Verlaine, Baudelaire, Hugo et al — tended to enhance the sensation on which he was concentrating. In Gallé's work, as in symbolist poetry, the evocation of a nuance of feeling or sensation was more important than practical purpose.

Most of Gallé's effect was gained through the surface, either through engraving, colour, etching with acid or inlaying other materials. However, the plasticity of his *marquetrie-sur-verre* encouraged a more three-dimensional approach to glassware. With the encrustation of relief, his vases gained a more animated silhouette. In his later work he began the final stage of experimenting with the actual shape of the glassware itself, rather than just the surface, so that whole new Art Nouveau forms were created.

Gallé's great success as a designer created its own

ABOVE LEFT: *Daum vase with poppy relief.*

ABOVE FAR LEFT: *Gallé here applies poured marquetrie-de-verre to a translucent vase engraved with irises, a favourite flower.*

difficulties in production as his career progressed. His reputation rested upon a limited production of works on which an enormous number of man hours had been concentrated. With increased demand, Gallé was persuaded to increase the capacity of his works by developing larger scale production, while simultaneously retaining a more exclusive hand-crafted output. The more numerous workshop designs inevitably lacked the degree of finish of his earlier work, but with a larger enterprise Gallé was able to expand his market, opening showrooms in London and Frankfurt, and ending his career as an employer of three hundred workers.

Gallé led a great renaissance of the glass industry in Nancy. The brothers Auguste and Antonin Daum, like Gallé, had taken over their father's workshop and begun to experiment with the new techniques to produce work in the Art Nouveau style. The Daum brothers were able to employ some of the talented designers working at Nancy, such as the versatile Jacques Gruber, and produced work very much in the Gallé manner. They too were concerned with opacity, colour and relief, using acid to eat away layers of glass to reveal hidden colour beneath and create delicately-modu-

lated backgrounds for relief work, or powdered enamel fused onto the surface in the furnace to create a glowing, opaque finish in a variety of colours.

The Daum brothers were also involved with the development of glassware produced by the more lengthy process of using pre-manufactured ground-down glass as an ingredient. By this means, and by the manipulation of oxidation to add the desired colour, an opaque form of glass, pâte-de-verre, could be produced, similar in appearance to alabaster. The technique had been known to the ancient Greeks and Romans, but was subsequently lost. Its rediscoverer, Henri Cros, used pâte-de-verre as a sort of mock marble, executing reliefs and free-standing pieces on a small scale, in a vaguely classical style. After Cros's rediscovery in the mid 1880s, pâte-de-verre began to interest Art Nouveau designers. The Conches craftsman, François Emile Décorchement, became the greatest specialist, but the Daum workshop also produced some designs by one of its employees, Alméric Walter. Walter perfected his pâte-de-verre technique at Daum before setting himself up producing statuettes in the medium.

Gallé's most important French contemporary in

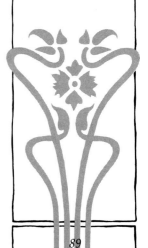

ART NOUVEAU

●

ABOVE RIGHT: *A Daum vase continuing the light and relief effects begun by Gallé.*

BELOW RIGHT: *Daum nightlight. The combination of glassware and artificial light was irresistible to the Art Nouveau.*

terms of experimentation and innovation was Eugène Rousseau, who began his career as an art dealer before starting up as a craftsman himself. The same year that Gallé exhibited his 'clair de lune' glass, Rousseau created an equivalent sensation with his Japanese-style glassware. He went on to become a technical pioneer; like Gallé, he used reliefs, inscriptions, tracery crazing in the glass, gold leaf and flecks. His most original work was using glass to imitate the texture and colour of gemstones. These appeared to be set into the glass vessel, but were themselves also made of glass. This work was continued by Ernest Léveillé.

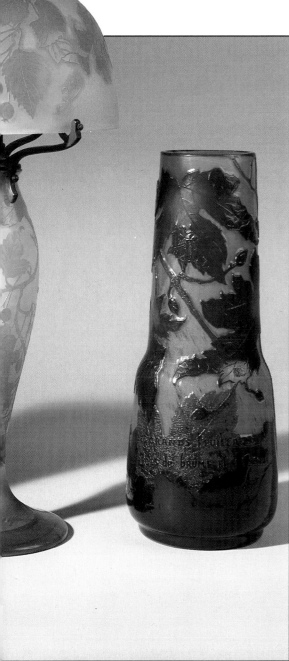

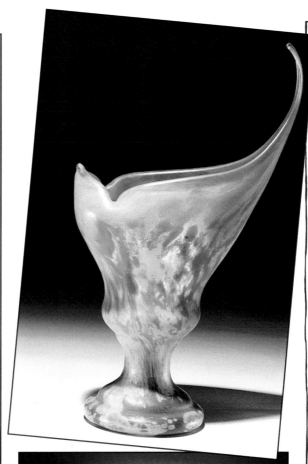

CENTRE: *Gallé lamp and orchid vase with (right) inscribed vase by Rollinant.*

ABOVE LEFT: *Daum glass chalice.*

BELOW LEFT: *Gallé lamp with overlay of butterfly and sycamores.*

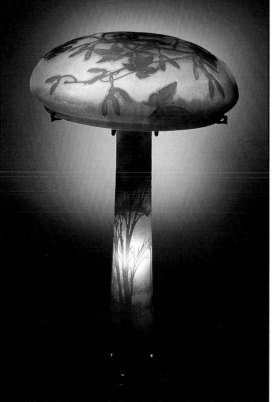

The great maestro René Lalique turned to glassware in the early years of the 20th century. He continued working in glass for the rest of his career becoming a leading designer of the Art Deco style which developed between the wars. Lalique's approach was directly opposed to that of Gallé, whose work was based on finishing the piece by hand. Lalique concentrated from the outset on large-scale production. All of his techniques had to be adapted to this basic need. From 1907, he began producing his famous perfume bottles, which used the colouring techniques of his Art Nouveau colleagues.

TIFFANY

RIGHT: *'Goose-necked' vase by Louis Comfort Tiffany, inspired by a Persian perfume flask.*

CENTRE *Tiffany lamp combining mosaic, bronze and coloured leaded glass.*

OPPOSITE ABOVE: *Glass plate by Louis Comfort Tiffany, again using the favourite peacock feather theme.*

OPPOSITE BELOW: *Tall Tiffany favrile glass, using the peacock feather motif, a favourite Art Nouveau device.*

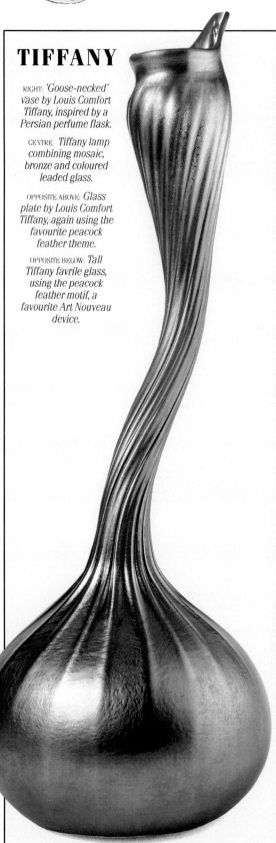

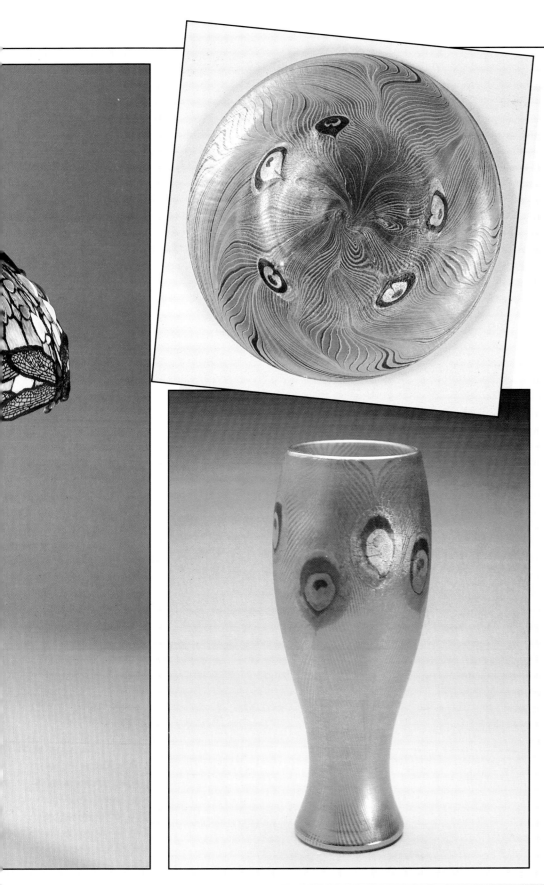

Louis Comfort Tiffany was the American designer who rivalled Gallé as a craftsman in glass. Tiffany came from a family of goldsmiths and jewellers and produced work in both these media, but after a study trip to Paris he began concentrating upon glassware. The Tiffany Glass & Decoration Company, founded in 1879, rapidly became a very successful enterprise, its most prestigious commission being the decoration of rooms in the White House. With the opening of a new glassworks at Corona, Tiffany began producing what he called Favrile, or hand-made glass goods. These exploited the use of chemical soaks or vapours to create different surface textures from matt to a burnished glow, and a variety of rich colours. Tiffany's glass rarely has the modelled plasticity of Gallé or Daum; its decoration, more abstract in its depiction of natural forms, rarely rises out in relief but appears to be more of an applied surface pattern. The silhouette of a Tiffany vase thus remains simple and elegant, although to complement the simplified decoration the vase shapes themselves are more adventurous, often stretched up on impossibly slender, plant-like stems or with twisting serpentine necks inspired by the works of the ancient Persian craftsmen. Unlike the Nancy School, Tiffany's glass never attempts to imitate gems, water, petals or any of other natural objects. Like Gallé, Tiffany's success encouraged a crop of imitators, chief among whom were the Quezal Art Glass & Decorating Company of Brooklyn, and Handel & Company of Connecticut.

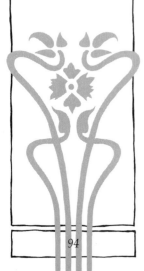

The development of the incandescent electric lamp by Thomas Edison in the 1880s posed a new challenge for designers. Tiffany was one of the first to realize the potential of electricity for the Art Nouveau style, and soon his name became synonomous with a style of lamp which used coloured, glass set into leaded panels exactly like a conventional stained glass window. The glass shades were either designed as flowers in a conventional shape, or, as in the Wisteria Lamp, each fragment of glass was a leaf in the foliage of a tree-shaped lamp whose trunk and roots were formed by the moulded metal of the stem and base. The opportunity for mixed media work in metal, ceramic and glass gave the electric lamp an instant appeal for the Art Nouveau, quite apart from the bright, even light that could be harnessed as part of the composition. It is typical of a tendency in Art Nouveau that the modernity of the electric light, its startlingly technological aspect heralding a new age, was ignored by many designers. Instead, filtered by coloured glass, its light became a gentle glow, a part of the idyll of lilies, swans and butterflies that kept the fantasy of an Art Nouveau interior unsullied by brutish technology. The treatment of the electric lamp in the hands of Tiffany or Gallé is exactly parallel to the use of wrought iron in the architecture of Horta or Guimard: it is used willingly but, although playing a major part in the whole, is masked by its conversion, against its very manufactured nature, into the organic world of Art Nouveau.

Both Gallé and Daum produced lamps of a very similar style to their other glassware. Glass figured as both base, neck and shade, and, typically, the form of a mushroom was quickly used as the most analagous form in nature. Other table, bracket and standing lamps used more metalwork, but the plant form naturally remained. In designs by Majorelle, Guimard, Gallé or Vallin, sinuous metal plants or saplings are created which flower into electric bulbs. The electric light is used in the same manner as the precious stone in a piece of Art Nouveau jewellery: the whole setting, whether it is a vine, thistle, a sprig of mistletoe or a lily, constitutes the bulk of the work, while the electric globes are scattered around the metalwork as highlights. While the majority of Art Nouveau lamps feature glowing flowers, the bronze or gilt statuettes of nymph-like figures produced by many craftsmen could also be adapted to carrying an electric light, providing rather a coy interplay between ornamentation and function. These lightly-draped females supporting desk lamps are perhaps an indication of Art Nouveau's retreat from the challenge of a new medium. They have an escapist charm, but to the eyes of a future generation of designers they would show only a retreat into impractical fantasy, at odds with the nature of the artefact itself. From the range of Art Nouveau craftsmen and designers only Henry van de Velde, commissioned by Bing, produced an electric lamp that took as its starting point the practical and scientific nature of the medium.

A more traditional part of glass design was that of stained glass. A huge revival of interest in the design and manufacture of stained glass had accompanied the Gothic revival, and it continued to be an important art form with the medievally-inspired English Arts and Crafts movement. The Art Nouveau treatment of stained glass grew from this revival and profited by the growing decorative similarities between stained glass, embroidery and painting. The first two crafts, by their very nature, were concerned with two-dimensionality, and, taking a cue from the crafts, painters of the 1890s in France were also concentrating on the

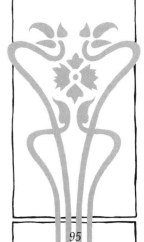

flat, decorative arrangement of colour in their works. Thus for Art Nouveau, stained glass was not so much a revivalist anachronism but a medium that was perfectly suited to the flatness, linearity and love of light and colour that were common to all the contemporary decorative arts. Also, a designer often wanted to control the light cast on his interior by making it harmonize with the flowing plant forms of the furniture, wallpaper and table ornaments. Tiffany even saw a useful social role in stained glass. In an age when many city dwellers were looking out onto a bare blank wall, a stained glass window could shield its owner from such a brutal sight and go some way to provide him with an idyllic world of flowers, birds and butterflies to gaze into instead.

Stained glass was widely manufactured and used to some degree in every wealthy home of the period, yet most Art Nouveau stained glass was not representative of a high level of craftsmanship, but consisted of regularly shaped, painted or enamelled panes, easy to produce and assemble. Only in the best quality designs was the traditional method of production retained, in which each motif was carefully outlined in lead, using panels of differing shapes and sizes. In Nancy, Jacques Gruber produced his stained glass of exquisitely-observed plants, flowers and birds in this way, as did Guimard in Paris. Guimard's stained glass, like his ironwork was designed as part of an architectural whole, and one sees in his windows the same abstract arches, bows and ripples as can be seen in the ironwork of his gates. The Swiss Eugène Grasset, who was also based in Paris, produced stained glass designs which were more traditional in subject matter than Guimard's, being very strongly related to contemporary graphic art, with Art Nouveau maidens idling in beautiful summer landscapes.

●

RIGHT: *Jacques Gruber window from the medical school at Nancy*

ABOVE LEFT: *Austrian Art Nouveau glassware by (left to right) Zasche, Powlony and von Harrach.*

BELOW FAR LEFT *Irridescent glassware c.1902 by the famous Austrian glass designer Richard Bakalowits of Austria, using intricate metal settings.*

BELOW LEFT *Window by Georges de Feure. The elegant and alluring female derives from the work of Aubrey Beardsley and relates strongly to de Feure's graphic work.*

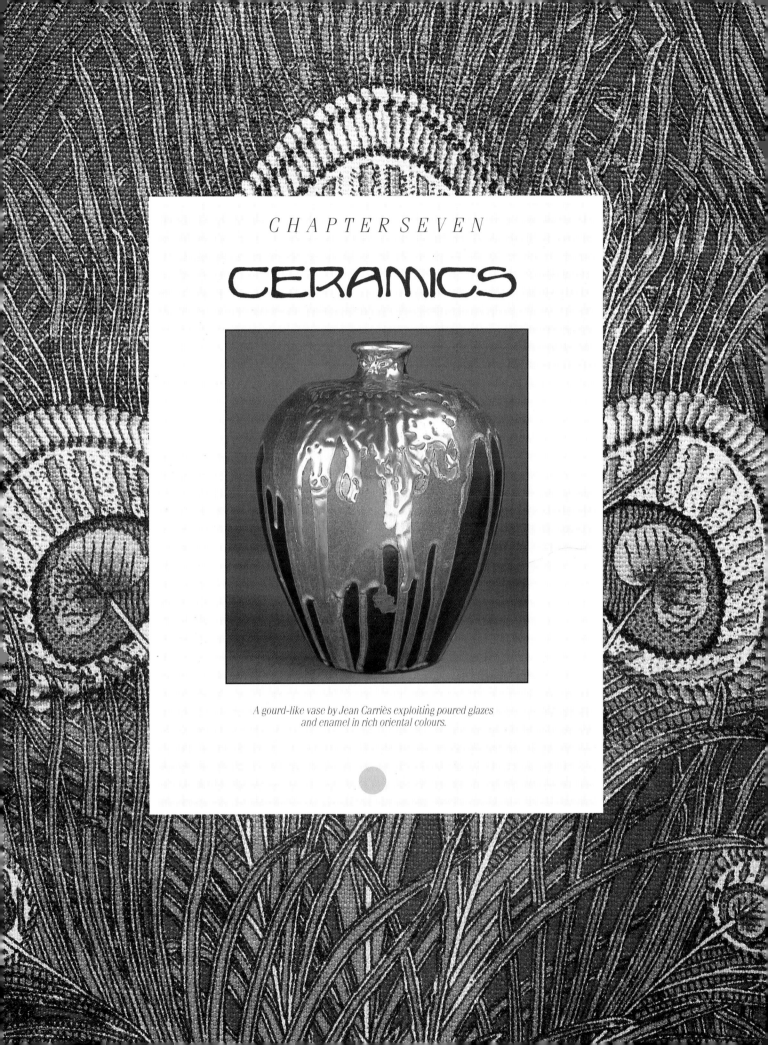

C H A P T E R S E V E N

CERAMICS

*A gourd-like vase by Jean Carriès exploiting poured glazes
and enamel in rich oriental colours.*

The divide between favouring individually-produced pieces and the volume production of factories was as great for the Art Nouveau ceramicist as it was for the glass craftsman. The two crafts were closely linked in both style and technique. Much the same kind of ware was produced in each medium and in both crafts the innovations of Art Nouveau increased the colour range and the possibilities for relief decoration, as well as changing the actual shape of the piece itself. However, whereas glassworks and metalworks tended always to be located in existing industrial centres because of the type of materials needed and processes involved, a pottery was a much smaller-scale establishment and in effect more 'portable'. The potter is only really concerned with a suitable clay, which can be obtained in a variety of locations. Pottery, at one level a commonplace and inexpensive necessity, had been produced in many small centres in both Europe and America. The craft tradition, on which the Art Nouveau revival was built, was widely spread, and a very large amount of ceramic wares were produced at many scattered provincial, and often rustic, centres.

This was particularly true of France, which was the centre of Art Nouveau ceramics. While their fellow craftsmen were concentrated mostly in the major centres of Paris and Nancy, and therefore had strong links with an entire cultural milieu, the Art Nouveau ceramicist often worked in isolation, in modest circumstances, and was therefore closest to the humble tradition of the potter. Gallé, de Feure, Colonna and others worked in ceramics too, but often their work was more closely linked with the major porcelain factories. These factories had acquired impressive new technology, but in terms of design creativity they had become stagnant. The new generation of artist-craftsmen turned their backs on fine porcelain almost entirely. Instead, they concentrated upon the production of more coarsely-grained traditional stoneware which was the subject of an enormous revival in the Art Nouveau period. The link between these innovators and their medium was strong enough in the public mind for their work to be simply and almost universally referred to as 'Art Pottery', neatly summarizing the designers, their medium and clientele. The artistic revival of stoneware created, throughout Europe and America, a whole new or revived tradition quite separate from that of porcelain production, and one that is still thriving today. The choice of a more 'democratic' medium was naturally not unselfconscious. It was very much influenced by the socially-conscious side of the Arts and Crafts movement that preferred plainer, cheaper materials that were free of associa-

tion with wealth and social aspiration. The exploration of stoneware had begun before the style of Art Nouveau was fully formed, yet it was primarily those working in the Art Nouveau manner that were responsible for developing the full potential of the medium. The same increased range of materials, exploring those that were hitherto seen as somehow inferior, has been noted in Art Nouveau metalwork and jewellery. The stress on aesthetic, rather than economic, criteria is entirely characteristic of Art Nouveau.

Despite its social implications, it is arguable whether the revival of stoneware would have been so significant if it had not been for the example of oriental, particularly Japanese, ceramics. The stylization, elegance and technical virtuosity of the oriental craftsman was once again an inspiration to their Art Nouveau cousins. Chinese porcelain had a very major impact on the west from the 18th century onward, and among aesthetes, such as Whistler and Wilde, there was a reverential enthusiasm for blue-and-white porcelain, although working craftsmen were more excited by the greater range of technical possibilities explored in oriental stoneware. Warm, rich colours

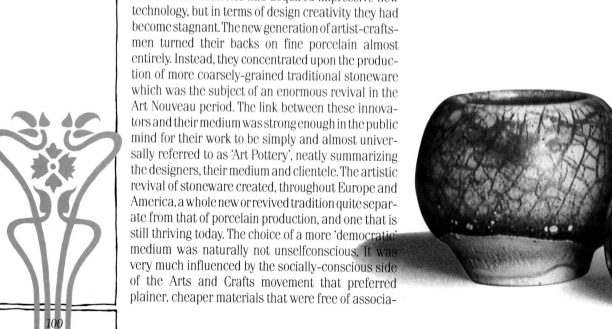

were possible, as were a variety of lustres, chance effects of liquid clay and glaze and a great range of textures, from porous roughness to cold, smooth glazes. All these areas were explored by Art Nouveau craftsmen. Art Nouveau's ambivalent, but important, relationship with scientific developments was also of significance for ceramicists. Advanced technical equipment and knowledge made new artistic effects possible in the crafts. An Art Nouveau variation of the artist-craftsman was the scientist-artist-craftsman typified in England by Dresser, in France by Gallé, Grasset, and Guimard's ceramicist-collaborator Alexandre Bigot, who was a professor of physics.

The Haviland workshop supported the works of pioneering French ceramicists. Originally established at Auteuil, it moved to the centre of Paris in 1881, where it was managed by Ernest Chaplet. Chaplet had been an apprentice at the state-owned Sèvres porcelain factory.While running the Haviland workshop, he rediscovered the technique for producing the much-envied *sang-de-boeuf* (oxblood) glaze of Chinese stoneware, which was as it name implies, deep red in colour. The secret of this process was something that Chaplet never divulged, but versions were developed by contemporaries, such as Adrien-Pierre Dalpayrat, the inventor of the similar, copper-based 'rouge Dalpayrat'. In 1887, Chaplet sold Haviland, moving to Choisy-le-Roi to continue his research. Here he developed a greater range of finishes — pitted, veined, dappled or polished. Chaplet's pupil and collaborator was Albert Dammouse who trained as a sculptor before devoting himself to ceramics. He was involved with Chaplet's innovations and also developed his own distinctive translucent paste. As one of the most talented of the new generation of ceramicists Dammouse was invited to use a studio for his experiments at the Sèvres works in 1892, because the directors, realised the need for some stylistic innovation in their rather conservative output. Ownership of Haviland passed from Chaplet to Auguste Delaherche. Delaherche developed one of the most distinctive motifs of Art Nouveau ceramics, the use of a drip glaze poured over the object. This was

A selection of vases and bowls by Ernest Chaplet, showing the range of finishes and forms he pioneered.

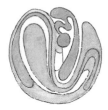

●

ABOVE RIGHT: *English Minton tiles with an Art Nouveau motif. Ceramic tile design had been revitalised by Morris & Co, and the Art Nouveau tiles were popular as a way of introducing further colour into the interior.*

ABOVE FAR RIGHT: *Minton tile with stylized floral decoration, c.1880-1900.*

BELOW RIGHT: *Stoneware vessel by Christopher Dresser. The use of a sea urchin is typical of the interest in the more unusual natural forms.*

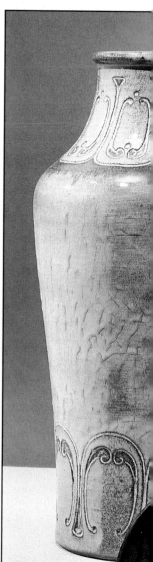

used by almost every ceramicist of the period and was a technique, once again, derived from the orient. The long, flowing curves of the poured glaze, its sense of vitality and almost organic growth, made it an enormously attractive technique for the Art Nouveau.

Although both Chaplet and Delaherche came from artisan backgrounds, a great painter was equally responsible for the development of an Art Nouveau style in ceramics. This was Paul Gauguin, whose influence over the whole area of decorative arts at the time was enormous. Gauguin experimented with ceramics at Haviland under both Chaplet and Delaherche, producing work free from the conventions that seem natural to the specialist but foreign to an artist from another discipline. Gauguin's ceramics appear rather crudely produced in comparison to the later, sleeker works of the Art Nouveau, but a certain primitive

coarseness was exactly the aim of his art at this time. Moreover, Gauguin's lack of inhibition in handling the clay resulted in haphazard budding, swelling and flowing forms with gnarled and twisted handles, and relief work taking the form of branches or some other less well-defined growth. These works, few in number, were produced in the late 1880s, both before and after Gauguin's trip to Martinique, and predate the development of the Art Nouveau proper of the 1890s. The Haviland workshop is of great significance for the development of Art Nouveau ceramics, technically through the innovations of Chaplet and Delaherche, and stylistically through Gauguin's experiments.

A parallel centre for stoneware production developed at Saint-Armand-en-Puisaye in the Nivernais region. The School of Saint-Armand focused on the charismatic and short-lived figure of Jean Carriès, who died at the age of 39. Jean Carriès discovered oriental stoneware in the collection of his friend Paul Jeanneney, who was to follow him to Saint-Armand and start producing orientalist ceramics. Carriès established himself in the local manor house and began exploring the range of coloured glazes for stoneware and the chance effects of poured enamel. His most distinctive work relies more on his training as a sculptor, for he also produced small figures and reliefs of grotesque faces and animals reminiscent of the extraordinary fantasies of the 16th-century Mannerists. These rather bizarre creations are some of the best examples of the fanciful and almost surreal side to much of the Art Nouveau borrowings from nature. Like metalwork, ceramics shares some common ground with sculpture, and the production of figurines or busts of the Art Nouveau nymph were as common in terracotta as they were in bronze. High-relief ceramic tiles, depicting aquatic creatures, mermaids, insects or birds, were also common as both interior and exterior decoration, as, for instance, those produced by Bigot for Guimard.

After Carriès death, his manor house was taken over by Georges Hoentschel, a versatile and successful designer who managed his own company. Inspired by Carriès, Hoentschel had moved to Saint-Armand in order to concentrate upon ceramics, and he continued to produce simple yet elegant ware enlived by the flowing lines of dripped glaze. Hoentschel also incorporated a great deal of floral detail into his vases. As in Art Nouveau glassware, this had the effect of breaking up the austerity of the silhouette by creating a more active contour. Hoentschel also used ormolu mounts for some of his pieces, immediately evoking roccoco precedents and emphasizing the sophistication of his work. In this respect Hoentschel's work is closer to

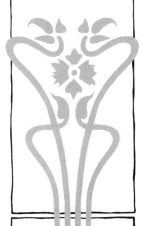

RIGHT: *Auguste Delaherche vase with a blue drip glaze and the almost ubiquitious peacock feather motif.*

FAR RIGHT: *Vase by Adelaide Robineau. The form and decoration of Art Nouveau continues here into a piece of stoneware from 1921.*

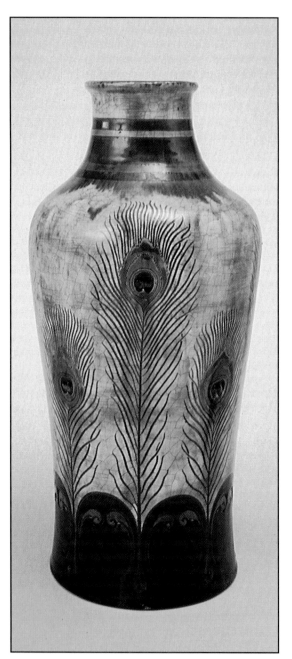

that of the Nancy school, such as Gallé and Majorelle, whose own work combines the glazes of the oriental style with the natural detail and intricate relief of the Nancy style as a whole. Gallé's work in particular, has a characteristically opulent air to it in contrast to the humble associations of stoneware. Insects or flowers might be picked out in gold and the colours were the brighter hues of faïence.

Somewhere between the rugged texture of stoneware and the bland finish of porcelain was the shimmering warmth of lustreware. The rich glow of lustreware glazes have an affinity with glassware, either the

matt finish of Tiffany's favrile vases or the opaque sheen of *pâte-de-verre*, emphasizing the closeness of the two media. The Messier workshop was the main producer of French lustreware, designed by the artistic director of the works, the noted Art Nouveau painter Levy-Dhurmer.

Stimulated by improving standards and increasing popularity, the two great state-controlled porcelain factories of Sèvres and Limoges forged links with established Art Nouveau designers. Apart from encouraging Edouard Dammouse's work, the Sèvres factory commissioned work from other designers

●

LEFT: *A selection of pierced stoneware vases by Auguste Delaherche.*

BELOW RIGHT *Sèvres vase showing a tentative response by the State French porcelain manufacturer to the natural detailing and elongated forms of Art Nouveau.*

BELOW FAR RIGHT *Vase by Taxile Doat, probably produced before his departure for America.*

independent of the company, including Guimard. Guimard's ceramic designs were well suited to porcelain for, rather than focusing on a natural warmth, texture and colour indentifiable with stoneware, they were essentially hard-lined, abstract, linear creations carried onto three dimensions, in which the rising curve of the vase's silhouette is incorporated into the composition. Georges de Feure and Edward Colonna designed for Limoges, an apt combination since both were sophisticates well versed in the eighteenth century style, which had been a strong influence upon the elegance of their interiors for Bing.

Taxile Doat was a ceramicist who made his name

working at Sèvres while continuing an independent production of his own. Doat treated porcelain to the techniques of the stoneware innovators using dripped glazes and even the vegetable shapes of gourds, marrows (squash) and pears, which had been used at Saint-Armand. He also varied the texture of his work by having *pâte-sur-pâte* medallions, like ancient cameos, applied to the surface, which proved to be popular. Doat increased his reputation by the publication of *Grand Feu Ceramics*, a treatise on the new techniques of firing and glazing. The book was read with interest in the United States, in particular by the entrepreneur Edgar Gardner Lewis. Lewis was a dynamic

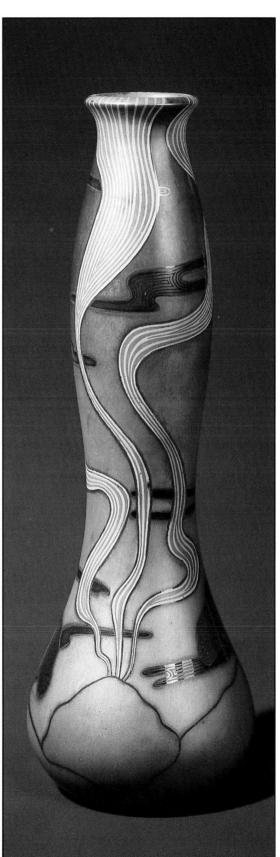

LEFT: *Stoneware vase by Joseph Rippl-Ronai for Zsolnay of Hungary. Maintaining the essentially fluid style of Art Nouveau, the Hungarian variation introduced a distinctively central European element to forms and colour.*

FAR LEFT *Ceramic bust by Gustave Obiols. The dreamy Art Nouveau maiden returns, this time in clay.*

figure, instrumental in founding the Women's League and the Art Institute of the People's University of University City, Missouri. Offered a fine supply of clay and the enthusiastic backing of the amateur potter Lewis, Doat left Sèvres in 1909 to work at the University City Pottery.During his five-year stay, Missouri stoneware gained an international reputation.

An enormous number of potteries opened up in America between the Philadelphia Centennial Exhibition,which introduced Arts and Crafts ideas in 1876, and the Chicago World's Fair of 1893. The development of American ceramics ran parallel to experimentation with the use of exotic glazes on simple stoneware shapes that occurred in France. The Robertson family of the Chelsea Keramic Art Works developed slip glaze decoration and an American version of the *sang-de-boeuf* glaze. In Cincinnati, Mary Louise McLaughlin, a gifted amateur, produced similarly pioneering work as did the commercial Rockwood Pottery in the same city. The Art Nouveau style was seen to some degree in the elegant, elongated vase forms and curving plant-like handles, but more particularly in the inlay of sinuous lilies, orchids and other Art Nouveau favourites. Newcomb College Pottery of Tulane University, New Orleans provided fine examples of this approach to ceramic design.

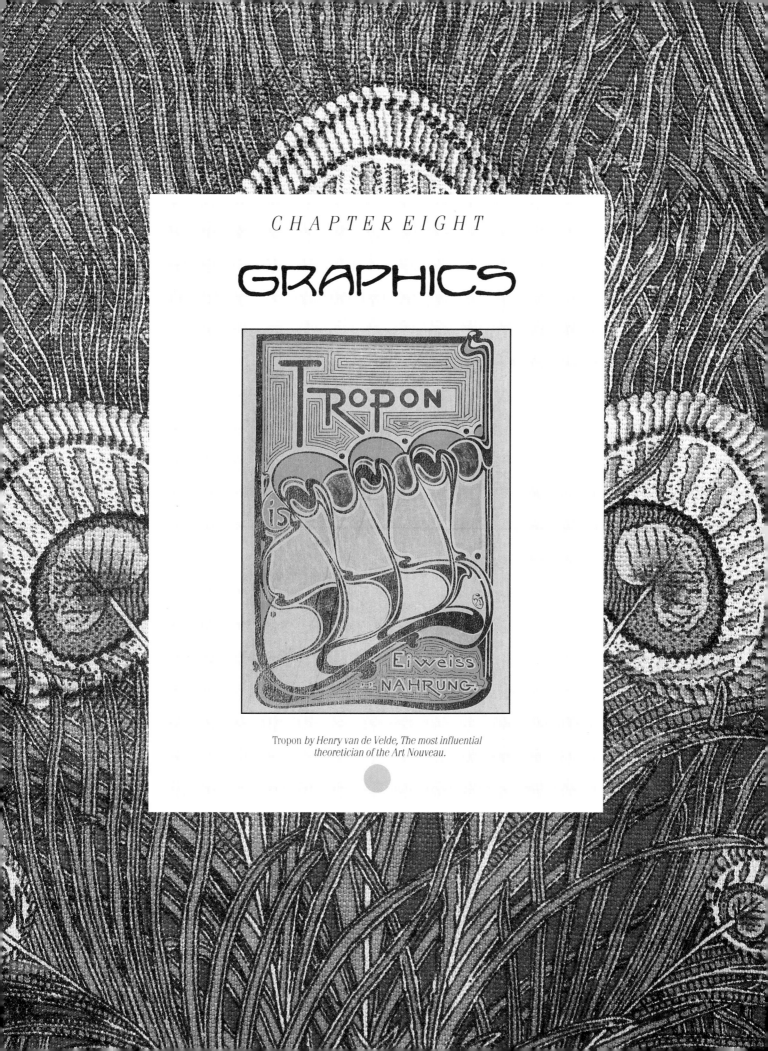

CHAPTER EIGHT

GRAPHICS

Tropon *by Henry van de Velde, The most influential*
theoretician of the Art Nouveau.

RIGHT: *The title page of Eugène Grasset's* Histoire des Quatre Fils Aymon.

The Art Nouveau style found its most complete expression in the graphic arts. The emphasis on line, the whiplash line of a plant stem, a swallow's wing or woman's hair was clearest in a medium in which line was the principal, or only, element. In every other medium the Art Nouveau artist was most successful when he was able to concentrate upon linear elements, whether it was in the design of a wrought iron balcony or stained glass. Book illustration, poster design and typography were all media in which the demands of mechanical reproduction limited the possibilities for nuances of tone, colour, atmosphere and light, which are the tools of the painter. Instead, the graphic artist concentrated upon strength of design and linear inventiveness. The strongest design was very often that which acknowledged the flatness of the medium, and therefore concentrated on patterning the surface. Ironically, this was also the style of avant-garde French painting of the 1880s and 1890s, particularly of Gauguin and his followers and the transition from fine to decorative art was easier to make at this time than at any other in the nineteenth century. It was in some ways paradoxical that the increasingly abstract and decorative tendencies of painters had an influence on the discovery of the essentially decorative element in the graphic arts.

It was natural that Symbolism, as a movement involving both painters and writers naturally encouraged a meeting with Art Nouveau of the two via illustration. Literary themes and allusions were common

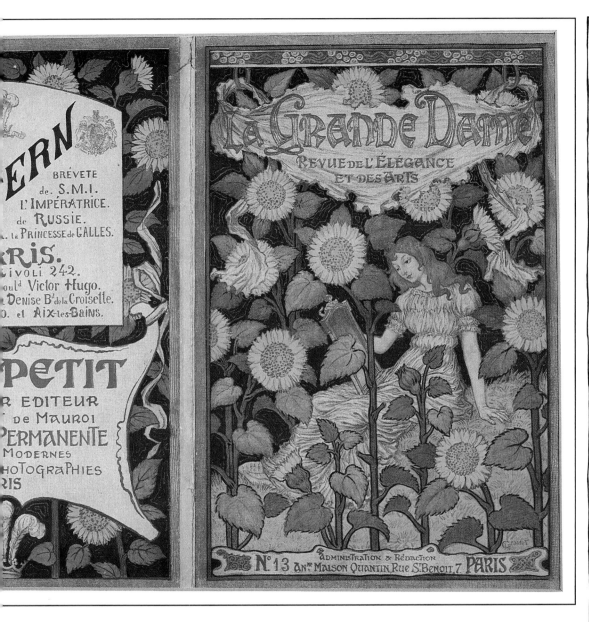

in painting and it was a small step to actual illustration, as practiced by Manet, Redon, Denis and others. This was part of a general drift away from realism in the arts to fantasy and stylization, the impulses behind Art Nouveau decoration. Combining visual images with text also resulted in a work that was more than a sum of its parts. It approached the mysterious, all-embracing work to which writers of the time aspired. The many references by writers, to painting, music and to the neglected senses of taste and smell, were used to enhance the breadth of their symbolist moods. Literary references could have a similar use in the arts and crafts. Gallé's *verre parlant* is perhaps the best example, using quotations to add a further dimension to his work.

This was the theoretical background but, for the illustrator, approaching a text with the aim of creating a unified work of art presented certain practical difficulties. The ideal was an integration between text and image rather than the use of a few isolated plates throughout the volume. This integration of various elements into an overall design was very much the forte of Art Nouveau. Made possible by the versatility of the designers involved, it has been clearly seen in interior design, where a uniform style involved even the smallest objects in a stylistic harmony with the whole. The fact that many of the leading Art Nouveau figures were literary figures too, frequently authors in their own right, naturally strengthened the visual and literary relationship.

●

RIGHT *Aubrey Beardsley
illustration to* Morte
d'Arthur. *Beardsley's
fantastic Art Nouveau
interpretation was far
removed from\ Morris'
medieval ideal.*

Book production was generally acknowledged to be of poor quality in the 19th-century. 18th-century typography styles and bindings were still being used in a rather debased form. In France, bibliophile societies were formed at an increasing rate as the century progressed in order to encourage higher standards of paper production, printing and binding. Limited deluxe editions were commissioned from craftsmen, parallel to the production of ordinary 'edition bindings' in larger quantities for the general public. The effect of this enlightened patronage was apparent only in terms of the quality of materials and binding. A corresponding improvement in artistic quality had to come from the designers themselves.

In 1891 William Morris turned his attention from interior design to the problem of artistic quality in book design. The first publication of his Kelmscott Press appeared in that year and the revival of the printed book began in earnest. Morris designed new typefaces, and used text and illustration as elements in an integrated page design. Morris's work was of great importance though the Arts and Crafts style did not develop an Art Nouveau curvilinear style. Arthur Mackmurdo's revolutionary title page to *Wren's City Churches* of 1883 had created a remarkable union of lettering and decoration in an Art Nouveau manner, but it was Eugène Grasset's production of *L'Histoire des Quatre Fils Aymon* in the same year which was the first totally integrated publication. Grasset had chosen a medieval legend and had spent over two years developing the decoration and illustration so that they became integrated, or even fused, with the text in a great variety of different ways. The actual style of graphics was not yet Art Nouveau but it was certainly derived from the sources that were to give it birth; flat areas and an emphasis on outline came from Japan and intricate patterned borders from Celtic illumination and carving. Grasset himself continued to be one of the most influential Art Nouveau illustrators and poster designers.

An important part of Grasset's subsequent work was the treatment of lettering itself as part of the whole design. This was far easier to do when the written element was limited, as in a poster, magazine cover or advertisement, and Grasset's creation of new forms was echoed by other artists in these fields. On a larger scale, Guimard had created his own lettering style for his Métro work to blend into his total composition. As in Art Nouveau as a whole, Art Nouveau lettering avoided the straight line as far as it was possible. Lines flowed into gently curving shapes and where they met they were looped together with intertwined tendrils. The intention was to remove the letters as far

HOW SIR TRISTRAM
DRANK OF THE
LOVE DRINK

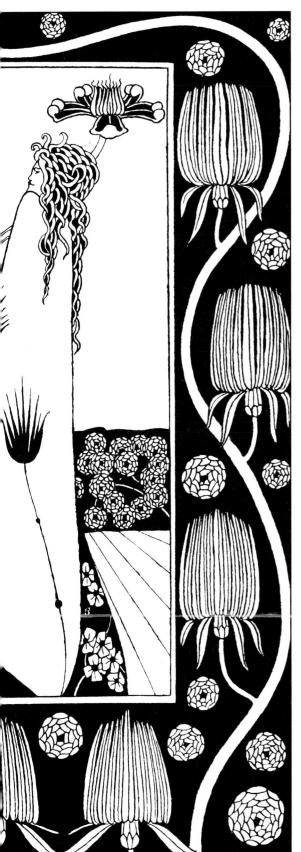

as possible from the idea of print and mechanical reproduction. Oriental calligraphy was the model: the Japanese and Chinese scribe had the freedom to adapt shapes and express himself by the nuances of his brushwork without losing meaning. By including poetry or criticism in a woodcut, and making it attractive by virtue of the beauty of the calligraphy and its disposal in relation to the overall design, Japanese art had also shown the West how image and script could be successfully combined. While most Art Nouveau designers created individual letter types to suit the commission, in 1898, Grasset progressed to create a complete typeface, the first in Art Nouveau, enabling the style to spread more easily into commercial art. In 1900, Grasset's example was followed by Eckmann, who designed the heavier, more moulded typeface associated with the Austro-German Jugendstil.

In England, the Arts and Crafts allegiance of most designers inhibited anything emphatically curvilinear in the graphic arts. Walter Crane's illustrations often exploit sweeping curves and rather intricate decoration, but even he later repudiated this tendency in his art. Despite the general climate, the greatest figure in Art Nouveau illustration developed in England during this time. This was the brilliant young illustrator Aubrey Beardsley, who began his career in 1893 illustrating *Morte d'Arthur* for Morris's Kelmscott Press. Morris was outraged by the result, rightly seeing it as a style antipathetic to that which he was trying to encourage, and this provoked an acrimonious dispute. Beardsley was developing his own highly personal version of the Art Nouveau style. He favoured asymmetry in the layout of the page, and natural detailing was stylized into essentially artifical and over-refined forms. Movement was conveyed through great unbroken, sinuous curves, and, most importantly, any sense of space was sacrificed in favour of a dramatic interplay between large simplified areas of black and white. Beardsley's sources were those of most Art Nouveau artists — the orient, an element of the medieval, an increasing fascination with the 18th century and a very distinctive re-intepretation of some early Renaissance decoration. Yet Beardsley's work is startlingly original, deriving most of its impact from his peculiar literary sense and the heightened sensibility of an invalid's delicate constitution. Beardsley was fascinated by the decadence of the time; his most characteristic illustrations are those for Oscar Wilde's *Salome*, in which he creates a world of cruelly perverse sensuality, of great visual refinement, exoticism and occasional sardonic wit. It has the studied amorality of the *fin-de-siècle* dandy epitomized by Beardsley and Wilde. Beardsley's sinister eroticism

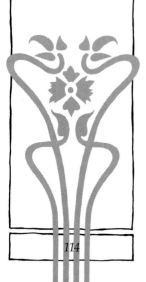

and cruel distortions were very distant from the freshness of much Art Nouveau flora and fauna, yet they were given form by the same sinuously active line, and had the same asymmetrical elegance.

The character of Beardsley's world was very much his own, and it fostered many imitators across Europe and America. The use of simple black and white, and areas of heavy decoration set against areas of space, was a technique that was easy to copy and provided a strong impact with great economy. Many of Beardsley's imitators were extremely derivative, but his style could be used intelligently as part of a broader synthesis; in the graphic work of the Glasgow Four, it was combined with the distortions of Toorop and their own stylized Celtic to create a very distinctive variation. Like every all illustrator's work, Beardsley's designs penetrated widely because in a book or magazine format they were very easily transportable and were available in large numbers. This was particularly true of Beardsley's work for the *Yellow Book*, the journal of the English decadents, and the *Savoy Magazine*. Beardsley died of consumption at the age of 26.

While typography and illustration were being revolutionized by Art Nouveau artists, bookbindings themselves were also being produced. Deluxe of editions of books were often produced in flimsy bindings to allow a wealthy owner to commission his own, and this demand was being satisfied by a growing number of leather craftsmen. Of these, René Wiener of Nancy was one of the most highly skilled. Flaubert's *Salammbo*, an exotic historical fantasy, provided the theme for his most spectacular binding, which was designed by Victor Prouvé and had enamel corners by Camille Martin. The cover is an elaboration of Art Nouveau themes — swirling veils, writhing snakes, a naked Salammbo with long, unbound hair, fish, flames, insects, all reduced to flat areas of glowing rich colour.

The development of posters in the nineteenth century created a whole new area for the graphic artist. By the end of the century poster art had become a vogue with its own collectors and galleries, its commercial aspects underplayed and its artistic value emphasized. This situation had been largely brought about by the pioneering work of Jules Chéret in the 1870s and 1880s. Chéret rejected the traditional format of the poster as a concentration of written information relieved by occasional illustrations, and instead concentrated upon one large, brightly coloured eye-catching image supported by the barest information concerning the actual event advertised. Chéret concentrated on the maximum possible impact since he knew his poster would be competing for attention with all the distractions of the surrounding street. He was forced to simplify — colours became strong, shapes simple and flat — and dynamic and exciting movement was conveyed purely through an active linear design. Chéret's images of lively gay dancing girls were admired by painters and designers alike and anticipated the simplifying trend of the Art Nouveau. Chéret's line was still a little hesitant and fractured, as in an Impressionist painting, and it was Eugène Grasset who created the Art Nouveau poster proper by using stronger outlines and more fluid contours. The flatness and outlining of Grasset's forms emphasized an affinity with stained glass design, which he also produced. Grasset's work concentrated upon the central image of all Art Nouveau graphic design — the wistful, willowy young girl whose long hair and loose clothing billowed out into fanciful, fluttering forms.

Grasset's strong sense of structure, his occasionally intricate patterning and his colour, paler and subtler than Chéret's, appealed more to an aesthetically-inclined audience than the more vivid and energetic, extrovert images of the latter, and formed the basis of the development of the Art Nouveau poster. After Grasset its best know exponent was Alphonse Mucha, a Czech-born painter of some obscurity before his first poster for Sarah Bernhardt, then appearing in 'Gris-

LEFT: *Dubonnet Aperitif advertisement from the Chéret studio. Chéret concentrates on one lively image with the minimum of lettering.*

RIGHT: *La Samaritaine -
Alphonse Mucha.
Advertising a vehicle
for Sarah Bernhardt,
Mucha successfully
adapts Hebrew-
inspired lettering into
the Art Nouveau style.
The red lettering
behind the head is in
real Hebrew.*

monda', made his name overnight. Bernhardt continued to patronise Mucha for her posters as well as for
the stage jewellery he began to design for Georges
Fouquet. Mucha based his whole career as a poster
artist upon his successful formula of reducing the poster to an elegant, narrow strip, featuring a single,
usually full-length, female, simplifying the structure
to a few simple forms and using complicated and
intricate patterns to ornament the surface. The pale
colouring and wealth of intricate detail demand close
attention in Mucha's work and make it the opposite of
Chéret's direct imagery. Mucha was particularly
skilled at synthesizing his enormous range of sources
for decorative motifs into some kind of exotic homogeneity that still managed to be very much of its time.
The only influence Mucha ever publicly acknowledged, with the confidence of its originality, was that of
the folk art of his native Czechoslovakia. This is indeed
much harder to detect than many more recognizable
sources: Japanese woodcuts, Arab and Moorish
decoration, Byzantine mosaics, Romanesque and Celtic interlacing, quite apart from the influence of such
contemporaries as Grasset. In his weaker moments,
Mucha seems to use these in what is almost a pastiche
of Art Nouveau, but elsewhere they are very skilfully
combined and bound together by flowing hair with an
active life of its own, or by carefully observed flowers
and foliage. Mucha's output was enormous throughout the 1890s. Apart from the more prestigious posters
for plays and exhibitions he was widely employed for
advertisements, and also produced independent graphic work, posters without a theme or event other than
Mucha's own creation. They relied increasingly on
scantily-clothed females until these coyly provocative
maidens effectively became pin-ups, under the guise
of being 'Spring', 'Music' or 'Night'. These images have
a fluid grace and light charm that is very much of its
epoch.

A more refined sensuality is offered by the elegantly, and fully-dressed ladies of Georges de Feure's
graphic works. Georges de Feure's interior designs
represent a very soigné form of Art Nouveau, moving
ever closer to classical 18th-century simplicity and
always adorned richly but with restraint. However,
before he began designing for Bing and before an
involvement with symbolist painting, de Feure (whose
real name, from his Dutch father, was van Sluyters)
had trained under Chéret. His graphic work has a
vitality that immediately recalls Chéret, rather than
his own work in the decorative arts. De Feure relied,
too, on the emphatic linearity of Grasset, but produced
much more animated work. His swooping line and
proclivity for bizarre dwarfish grotesques and exag-

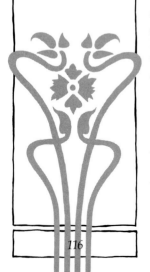

LEFT: *Palais Indiens Tea poster by Georges de Feure. An early de Feure with much of the uncomplicated good spirits of his master, Chéret. The mock-oriental motifs on the left-hand border show de Feure's graphic inventiveness.*

FAR LEFT: *Interior Scene, a gouache by Georges de Feure. A highly-sophisticated Art Nouveau scene featuring the furniture of the period as well as a Beardsley-inspired fascination with stylized female fashion.*

gerated costume details, best seen in his illustrations for Marcel Schwob's *La Porte des Rêves*, also reveal a strong debt to Beardsley. Like Beardsley, de Feure was more concerned with book and magazine illustration and covers than commercial advertising. His posters are concerned with galleries and exhibitions associated with his own style. The de Feure female of these works is generally a fur-coated, hatted, literary and artistic lady, refined, poised and closely related to her English cousin in the work of Beardsley.

In Holland, Jan Toorop had been involved in much the same quasi-mystical symbolist painting as de Feure. His images had blended fashionable eroticism and the occult with distorted, elongated forms derived from the shadow puppets of Java. It is one of the characteristic surprises of the Art Nouveau that such an artist could make the transition to advertising peanut oil as successfully as he did with his Delftsche Slaolie poster of 1895. Toorop's painting was certainly a geat deal more decorative than his rather portentious themes might suggest, and closer to the demands of commercial graphics. Yet examined from the other end of the spectrum, the poster is immediately identifiable stylistically with the most avant-garde type of painting in a way remarkable for a commercial poster of any age. It serves as atribute to the success of Art Nouveau in achieving some degree of unity across the arts and vastly increasing the artistic significance of what were hitherto banal media. Toorop uses the flow-ing hair of the two female figures to fill every available area of space in the design so the whole becomes a mass of hypnotically undulating rhythms.

Henry Van de Velde's Tropon poster, his only experiment in the medium, is comparable with Toorop's Delftsche Slaolie poster in its lack of stylistic compromise. Although an advertisement for a concentrated foodstuff, it is primarily an autonomous composition around the word 'Tropon' which makes no concessions to commercial concerns yet is unarguably striking and memorable. It almost has the right to stand as a work of abstract art in its own right and was certainly afforded a great deal of importance, then as now. Van de Velde holds to his rejection of the anecdotal natural detail of Mucha or Gallé. Instead, he concentrates upon shapes that suggest growth or liquid movement but cannot be tied down to any one source. Van de Velde's deeply held artistic ideals, of which this is one, and his socialist sympathies, would have made him a poor poster artist in commercial terms. He lacked Mucha's ability to adapt and develop a directly appealing subject matter for a variety for purposes, and so Tropon remains a brilliant but isolated example of his poster work. Instead, van de Velde's great graphic talent was concentrated upon a linear Art Nouveau style in other artforms. He had first started working in a purely graphic vein during a convalescence after his mental breakdown in 1889, that forced him to abandon his painting career. Graphic art was

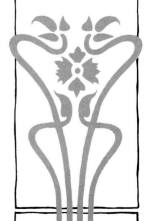

OPPOSITE: La Plume *calendar by Mucha. Mucha's treatment of hair as semi-abstract fronds is typical. Also notable are the jewellery, recalling his work for Fouquet, and the Egyptian motifs of the horoscope.*

ABOVE FAR LEFT *Bookplate by Koloman Moser. The combination of lively natural detail with an essentially orderly elegance is typical of the Viennese Secession.*

ABOVE LEFT: Reine de Joie *by Henri de Toulouse-Lautrec. Inspired by Chéret, the artist simplified the image still further by using flat, strong areas of colour. Lettering continues the active line.*

BELOW LEFT: Delftsche Slaolie *poster by Jan Toorop. Even the group of peanuts in the top left-hand corner of the poster have been endowed with an almost sinister Art Nouveau vitality, wriggling like amoeba.*

the path which led him to the Arts and Crafts movement and the ideals of Morris, reshaping his life to serve the social mission of an improved aesthetic standard in every branch of design.

The wide circulation of printed material ensured that graphic art was more easily seen in America than many other forms of Art Nouveau. Grasset also produced covers and illustrations for *Harper's Bazaar* and the *Century Magazine* in the early 1890s with great impact, particularly on Lhouis Rhead, an English immigrant who produced his first poster in 1890 and subsequently left to further his career in Paris. Rhead worked in the Grasset style and produced a cover for one of the prestigious Estampe Moderne portfolios of contemporary French prints. On his return to America, his Grasset style proved successful and he pursued a career in posters and magazine illustration. Will Bradley worked in Chicago and was self-taught, without the benefits of European travel. Like most American designers he based his style on the Arts and Crafts movement, but as an illustrator he was drawn toward the early Beardsley illustrations of *Morte d'Arthur.* Bradley employed the fluid line of Art Nouveau, separating the white and black of Beardsley, but retained a freshness and innocence almost entirely absent from Beardsley's later development. Bradley became sufficiently successful to publish his own occasional magazine, resoundingly entitled *Bradley: His Book.*

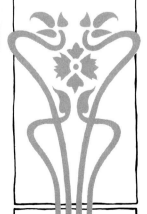

•

RIGHT: *Monaco, Monte-Carlo — Mucha. Railway travel to Monaco, supposedly advertised here, is downplayed in favour of an extravagant floral arabesque and an informally-clad, expectant young girl.*

LEFT: *Cover for Scribner's Magazine by Mills Thompson. One of the many occasional magazines that helped spread the Art Nouveau style through their graphic work.*

OCTOBER, 1902

ONE SHILLING

SCRIBNERS MAGAZINE

Mills Thompson '02.

CHARLES SCRIBNER'S SONS, NEW YORK. SAMPSON LOW, MARSTON & CO., Ltd., LONDON

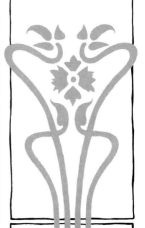

RIGHT: *The Inland Printer — Cover by Will Bradley. A design strongly influenced by Aubrey Beardsley.*

FAR RIGHT: *Griffiths Cycles by Tairiet. Strongly infuenced by Mucha, Tairiet here literally obscures the actual bicycle to concentrate on mobile feminine grace.*

CONCLUSION

The brief decade-and-a-half of the Art Nouveau style belies its importance in the history of art. The importance attached to the design of everyday objects began as an idea with William Morris and reached its zenith in the 19th century in Art Nouveau. It is still present today in the role of the designer in industry, shaping the goods that everyone uses. But some aspects of Art Nouveau now seem very distant: the florid exuberance of some decoration, the general insistence on hand-finished objects and a tendency to disguise the true nature of industrially-produced materials by wrapping them in plant forms, are all far removed from the style of 20th-century design. Modernity and tradition, science and nature, created tensions within Art Nouveau, and even in a style as homogeneous as Art Nouveau there were significant differences of outlook. On one hand, the French style was concerned with decoration as much as structure, was often ornate, owing a direct debt to the forms of nature, as well as to the artistic style of the eighteenth century. This was the style of the Nancy school, the Parisian decorators, and also of Horta, Toorop, Obrist, Endell and Tiffany. There was, too, a more sober side of Art Nouveau, concerned with structure and function, and the social role of art and the craftsman. This was the Art Nouveau of Van de Velde, Riemerschmid and Behrens.

The Art Nouveau of Van de Velde and the Austro-German designers gradually evolved into the first generation of twentieth-century style. The process was initiated first by Mackintosh and the Glasgow School, and second by the artists of the Viennese Secession and the Wiener Werkstätte. As has been seen, Mackintosh's style curbed the curving freedom of the Art Nouveau line within the elongated, rigid verticals of his architecture and furniture. He preferred plain black-and-white surfaces to natural grains and colour. Mackintosh's work, although in essence Art Nouveau, pointed the way to a possible future development of the style away from a greater proliferation of uncontrolled restless shapes.

The crafts revival came relatively late to Vienna. The arts and crafts group the Wiener Werkstätte, being formed only in 1903, 20 years after Mackmurdo's revolutionary designs. Hoffmann and Moser, the leading figures, were fascinated by Mackintosh's distinctive style and invited him to Vienna to exhibit with the group. The Wiener Werkstätte wholeheartedly embraced the Art Nouveau unity of the arts and the ideal of craftsmanship but what they actually produced, although undoubtedly extremely elegant and stylized, was increasingly based upon crisply organized straight lines rather than luxuriant Art Nouveau curves. Nor was there such an emphasis on natural forms, such as leaves and flowers. The group's main commission, the Palais Stoclet in Brussels, built by Hoffmann and decorated by his colleagues, has very little to connect it with the Art Nouveau that had originally fired the Viennese designers. The dining room was based around a frieze by the painter Klimt in his most ornate,

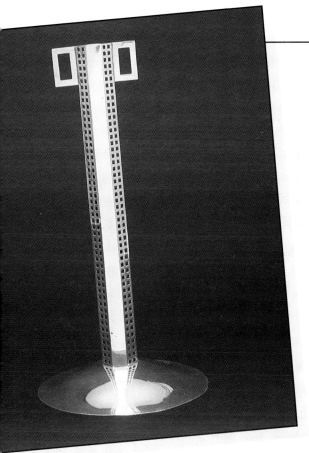

Art Nouveau manner, yet the furniture is severely simple plain and straight, as are the other fittings. The exterior of the house retains an Art Nouveau asymmetry and a rather fanciful tower, but is otherwise simple, restrained and undecorated. A similar reaction occurred in Paris where designers such as Gaillard, Colonna and de Feure were producing furniture of greater restraint and calm. However their designs were increasingly based on 18th-century prototypes and were sinking back into a kind of reworked revivalism. The Art Nouveau commitment to modernity continued with the designers of Austria and Germany, albeit in a new guise.

Van de Velde's influence on German Art Nouveau had been important. Through his visits, lectures and writings the ideas of a rational, functional form of design gained many followers. In 1899, the Grand Duke Ernst Ludwig of Hesse decided to form the artists' and designers colony of Mathildenhöhe at Darmstadt. Among those invited to move to Darmstadt was Van de Velde's disciple Peter Behrens, as well as Olbrich from Vienna. At Darmstadt, Behrens began to refine his Art Nouveau style into something simpler and more functional. In 1907, Behrens and Riemerschmid were influential in the foundation of the Deutscher Werkbund, a union of architects and designers based, in principal, on the Art Nouveau unity of the crafts but with the important difference of embracing the possibilities of industrial mass-production and designing according to these methods. With this revolutionary shift in attitude, Behrens was given an important task as a designer-in-chief to the great German electrical giant AEG. Behrens was responsible for all design, from products, to catalogues, company logo and factories. He thus became the first modern industrial designer of the 20th century and the first architect to seriously confront industrial architecture. Behrens' background as an Art Nouveau designer gave him the versatility to tackle such an enormous task whilst the enlightened offer of the post by the AEG director Paul Jordan was a tribute to the close ties between design and industry that had grown up in Germany during the Art Nouveau years.

Van de Velde himself had moved to Weimar in Saxony in 1901 at the invitation of Grand Duke Wilhelm Ernst of Sachsen-Weimar in order to improve the level of design and establish workshops for the production of fine quality goods in Weimar. By 1907 these workshops had become a state-run crafts school over which van der Velde continued to preside. The Weimar school was to develop in the inter-war years to become the Bauhaus, later to move to Dessau, and the single most important influence on 20th-century design. The flourishes and ornament of Art Nouveau vanished rapidly in the early years of this century but the stress on the importance of good design in crafts, and the encouragement of artists to develop as designers too, continued to influence the appearance of the everyday world.

INDEX